The Funny Thing About Being A Widow?

On A Dating Site

By

Sandra E Manning

ISBN 978-1-9162116-2-9

Editor Clare Solomon Meroda UK Editing

Book cover design by Samantha Santana
amaiddesigns.com

Contents

In Loving Memory

Of

Leyla Mae Bell

02.09.2021 to 14.01.2023

An extraordinary light destined to shine

Forever

Lucas Alexander Bell 23.06.2024

Take the hand of your sister darling boy and fly high with the angels

Introduction

When I wrote my first book **The Funny Thing About Being a Widow?** after the death of my husband in 2014, my aim was to illustrate how humour and laughter can be used during the process of grieving and need not be as incongruent with death as we tend to believe that it is. The reaction to the book was largely positive, considering its title was always going to divide popular opinion into two distinctly separate camps in a similar way to Marmite.

Laughter is a natural human reaction to something we find amusing in the same way that tears are when we find something sad. We have no control over these mechanisms and there is no right or wrong way to employ them, or at least there didn't used to be.

All too often nowadays I find myself wondering whether or not it is appropriate to laugh at something I would have giggled at one time over without a second thought. Increasingly, I feel the need to check whether or not the source of my amusement is on the growing list of things that we are not supposed to laugh at in case we cause offence. I doubt that I am alone in finding this a worrying and even disturbing trend.

Not unreasonably, given the titles of both my first book and now this one about widows on dating sites, I have been asked many times what it is that is even remotely funny about being a widow. My answer, as always, is absolutely nothing per se, but this does not mean that because we are widows or have been one we can't still appreciate humour even when it's at our own expense.

My late husband's appreciation of the benefits of enjoying a good laugh didn't just disappear after his cancer diagnosis. He may no longer have had any choice concerning his longevity beyond this point, but he was absolutely determined not to surrender his right to laugh about it when, and if he felt so inclined. Similarly, it was my love of laughter that saved my life when I lost him and, for that, I make no apologies ever.

Having included a chapter in my first book about my experiences of online dating, the reaction to it suggested that this was a subject worthy of the space allowed by a stand-alone volume in the series. Throughout my many years of speaking with widows and widowers, the question of when, if, and how one might go about seeking out another relationship, as a bereaved spouse, crops up with a greater frequency than any other question I get asked.

In this book, I have recorded the most relevant results from my time spent on four well-known dating sites to conduct what I loosely term my *research*. I conducted all my own stunt work during this process and elected not to use the services of a body double. I would like to provide assurances that, as far as I am aware, there was no damage caused to the eyesight of those who came into direct contact with the original as a result of this omission.

I have sought to provide information here that is both practical and empathetic when it comes to negotiating the very real hazards that can be encountered on dating sites. You will also find many examples of a blatant disregard for my own safety to which I would like to add the following disclaimer:

PLEASE DO NOT TRY THIS AT HOME.

My lifestyle is a world away from anything that could be described as opulent, but in the interest of keeping the canvas over my head, and not losing it to a litigious enthusiast, I have endeavoured to remove any identifying features from the anecdotes I have shared. The examples I have elected to include are by no means exhaustive but have been chosen because they ably illustrate some of the common scenarios you are likely to encounter on a dating site.

I repeat here, as I was at pains to point out in the introduction of my first book, that I am not an expert on anything but myself and my own life. That being said, it is my sincere hope that readers can relate to what I have to say in the pages that follow, if only to disagree with it.

My love of humour is as important in my life now as it ever has been. Without the ability to laugh at life and myself, I am sure I would be in a different place to the one I find myself fortunate enough to be in now. This is in no small part due to a dating site frequented by frogs, brain surgeons, astronauts and multi-millionaires with cash flow problems. Despite them all, at the time of writing this introduction in 2024, I will have been happily remarried for five years in September of this year. Given the route I took through this matchmaking quagmire, there are still days when I pinch myself that I was lucky to walk away from this experience having acquired a prince for the second time in my life.

I am reliably informed that the fifth year of our union is our wooden anniversary. The significance of this material in this context is said to be because wood has a durability which increases both in strength and beauty throughout the years. This is not information I intend to share with my husband, however, who would probably consider a chopping board to be a perfectly appropriate anniversary present in light of it. I have sourced a beautifully turned wooden mallet in case he should decide that this is a risk worth taking.

When I am asked if I could go back in time, would I still use the services of a dating site to find a new relationship, my answer is yes, I would. Finding my new husband was a welcome bi-product of a mechanism that I used without the singular intent of finding a new life partner, even if I wasn't opposed to it happening if I did.

Most of the things we hope to achieve in life require an investment of time, effort and hard work. We do not expect to walk straight into a well-paid job for instance, without either working our way up towards it or pursuing relevant qualifications that justify being paid a decent salary. Our expectations of dating sites, however, are somewhat less reciprocal in that we expect in exchange for a relatively small amount of cash, or even for free, that it will deliver us a suitably matched life partner, all with the bare minimum of effort on our part. When pursuing one of the most precious relationships we can ever hope to have, quite why we are reluctant to put in the same amount of time and effort that we take for granted is necessary to achieve anything else of value in our lives, is frankly beyond my comprehension.

Apart from co-founding GOWNS, an online support group for Grieving Overwhelmed Widows Negotiating Stuff, I am also a member of many other support groups where the subject of online dating sites is one of the most predominant topics of conversation. I am always saddened to hear of people's negative experiences on dating sites. Whether this is because of an encounter with a romance scammer or just as the result of finding out that you are not compatible with someone you had hoped to have a relationship with, it is understandably enough to discourage anyone from using them. For people who do decide to cut and run and elect to find other ways of leading happy and fulfilling lives without a partner this is, of course, always a personal choice. For some of us though, dating sites might be the only way in which we can feasibly expect to encounter a new relationship prospect. With some effort and perseverance, including a greater vigilance than my own errant exploits will go on to demonstrate, dating sites can be successful for some.

I have been fortunate that fate delivered the love of two wonderful men to my address, not once but twice during my lifetime. One of them was posted to me in the traditional way with a stamp and the option of returning to sender, and the other via an email routed through a dating site, which thankfully dodged potential oblivion in my junk mail.

It is not my intention to influence a widow or widower's decision to use or not to use a dating site as a result of what I have written in the following pages. My aims are simply to present the positives and negatives involved from the perspective of a bereaved spouse and as always to do this with my tongue firmly in my cheek.

Halt! Who goes there?

If you are not likely to be offended by the inclusion of some adult language that might have found its way onto the pages that follow then by all means proceed without further ado.

If the opposite is true, then this might be a good juncture at which to go and watch a re-run of the Waltons on the telly instead.

Chapter 1

A Fairy Tale Beginning

Once Upon A time

At 4.00 pm on a summer's day way back in another lifetime, the rain clouds parted and allowed a few watery slivers of light to peep through them, because this was a typically British summer that we are talking about. A young bride finally dared to hope that her wonderfully white wedding gown might remain so after all, as she stepped down from a sleek black limousine on the arm of her proud father.

Those memories of my wedding day on the 1st of July 1978 are etched in my mind with a clarity that has proved immune to the dulling effects of the forty or so years that have since elapsed.

As I took each step closer towards Kenny, my handsome future husband, I knew even then that I was walking into the adventure of a lifetime. I was barely aware of the presence of those who had gathered to witness our union, most of whom presumed that the reason behind our hurriedly arranged nuptials was the existence of a soon-to-be-announced pregnancy. Those who did not subscribe to this view were placing good odds on the likelihood that our marriage would not last much beyond our leaving the confines of the vestry on account of my tender young age. As someone who had been responsible for the care of my ailing mother for most of my childhood years, the suggestion that I lacked the maturity to understand the commitment I was now about to undertake, was something of an anathema to me.

As is often the case when champagne is quaffed with rare abandon, inhibitions tend to fade into obscurity. Shortly after the obligatory *First dance*, I was soon busting shapes that were more synonymous with that of a gymnastic environment. Unfortunately, I had forgotten that I had something tucked inside my not-so-virginal underwear which was now working its way free from their confines by courtesy of my contortions. In line with the time-honoured tradition that dictates a bride should wear something borrowed and something blue, Kenny had written several fairly graphic suggestions as to how we might spend our first night as man and wife on a piece of blue notepaper in acknowledgement of this long-held tradition. As the result of my continued gyrations on the dance floor, the notepaper made its final bid for freedom and ended up in the hands of our six-year-old niece, whose reading skills extended well beyond those of someone her age. Against the backdrop of a fading glam rock track, she began to demonstrate those skills by reading out loudly from the notepaper to an increasingly curious and amused audience.

With my train billowing behind me like a full sail on a catamaran, I launched towards the little cherub just at the point she was enquiring as to the meaning of the word *Tits* which I knew was relatively benign in the context of what was to follow it. Thankfully, my new husband was able to distract our niece with a packet of salt and vinegar crisps and a pound note before tucking the literal blueprint safely behind the carnation in his top pocket.

The 1st July 2016

Sadly, at the time of writing the above, almost two years after Kenny's untimely death at the age of fifty-seven, the anniversaries of our wedding are no longer the happy occasions they once were. Now that we can no longer exchange carefully considered gifts on our wedding anniversary, the only thing I can offer my darling husband in its place is the knowledge that I am doing okay. Despite a few detours and deviations, I am finding ways to negotiate the lonely path ahead of me without him by my side, and more than anything I want him to know that his legacy of love is now safe in my hands.

My darling Kenny

I miss you so very much each and every day, but never more so than on the days that have special meaning for us such as our anniversary today.

Yes, there are still times when it is very hard to stem the tears that threaten to cause a drought in my tear ducts. Nowadays though, when this happens, I allow them to fall freely just as they are doing now because I have learned that the rain on my face will dry and that the sun will shine through the clouds just as it did on our wedding day all those years ago. If the start of our wonderful adventure began with a very rude note written on some crumpled blue note paper, then the chapters that follow it have now become the subject of my books.

You were always so supportive of my musings on paper and often encouraged me to take them more seriously, although I doubt either of us would have predicted that my eventual excursion into the printed medium would be prompted by your departure.

I am not sure how busy things get where you are now, my darling, but it might be an idea to pull up a couple of chairs at some point and charge some glasses in readiness for the time that I finally run out of ink and we can have the mother of all catch-ups.

In the meantime, I wish you a Happy Anniversary darling, I will love and miss you for the rest of my life. Sandra xxxxx

When The Fairy Tale Goes Grimm

I hadn't looked into a full-length mirror for many years and, now that I was, the rationale behind this tactic of avoidance was depressingly clear. In common with a lot of women who have enjoyed long and happy marriages, I was inclined to take it for granted that I was both loved and desired. Now, as I took stock of the toll that many years of complacency had inflicted on my middle-aged form, I concluded that my late husband probably deserved a medal for his many acts of gallantry. Mounting the equivalent of what had come to resemble the North Face of the Eiger several times a week during a particularly active one, spoke volumes about his love and commitment.

Changing my stance in front of the mirror did little to nothing to improve the view. Although unrivalled in terms of comfort, the voluminous capacity of my underwear was comparable to that of a fully deployed parachute which had faded well beyond *Fifty Shades Of Grey.*

I was further irked to discover the presence of what are commonly described as *Bingo Wings* on the underside of each arm, despite rarely ever having played it. In the interests of conducting a full and proper disclosure, I turned my attention further south only to be further depressed by the fact that I needed both hands to hoist up the expanse of excess flesh that hung loosely around my lower abdomen. It was the fabulous Northern comedian Peter Kay who once described this feature as the *Canopy Over the Sweetshop*. The size of the canopy guarding the entrance to my *sweetshop,* was such that it wouldn't have been unreasonable to assume that it had been closed for business for some considerable time. Then there were the deposits of cellulite which clung to my thighs like lumps of out-of-date cottage cheese, not to mention the coarse black hair (a bit unfair for a blonde) that sprung like cacti from my legs and which would have taken an industrial depilatory cream to successfully dispatch.

Despairing by now that I would ever be able to locate at least one redeeming feature that might not pose a substantive threat to the sensitive workings of a cardiac pacemaker, I paused for a moment to consider that my face, once described as *pleasing,* by my grandmother, might just be it.

That was of course until I discovered that two of my chins had apparently invited another one round for a threesome during my period of inattention.

To say that I was utterly dismayed and angry with myself for allowing this unfavourable state of affairs to exist would have been something of an understatement, particularly now that it was also incredibly inconvenient.

During the slow and laborious process of re-engaging with the world, although obviously from a different perspective than before I lost Kenny, I became aware of the existence of *Catfishers* after taking a cursory look at dating sites. These are despicable fraudsters who prey on vulnerable people by assuming a bogus identity online, usually with the intention of gaining a pecuniary advantage. Researching further, I discovered that widows and widowers were overly represented amongst those who parted with sums of money sometimes representative of their whole life savings because of their perceived relationship with an online fraudster.

At this stage, if I am brutally honest, I had little to zero sympathy for those who fell victim to this form of *Romance Fraud.* It seemed incomprehensible to me that anyone could ever allow themselves to be duped in this way. My curiosity as to why this form of fraud succeeded was sufficiently aroused for me to decide that I would investigate the methodology used by these characters to help raise awareness of their criminal proclivities.

The recent consultation with my *Mirror Mirror On The Wall*, however, had thrown something of a spanner into those plans to conduct further research. Not only had it provided irrefutable evidence that I was not the fairest of them all, but that things were significantly worse than that. As things stood, my presence on an online dating site was likely only to be of interest to serial killers or men who still lived at home with their mothers.

Where Is Your Fairy Godmother When You Need Her?

There was no escaping the fact that, in order to achieve any of my research aims, I needed to take some drastic remedial action. The most pressing of the issues that needed to be addressed was that of my excess poundage. I tackled this by basically giving up eating and extracting the nutrients I needed from a range of high-protein shakes instead. The only problem with this method of losing weight is that the shakes tasted utterly revolting. Despite the fruity flavours in the range having delicious-sounding names such as *Banana Sublime* or *Strawberry Sensation,* the reality was that they all tasted like *Morinda Citrifolia,* more commonly known as vomit fruit. Thankfully, there was one flavour in the range that I did find tolerable which was the *Lovely Latte*. This I discovered became distinctly more lovely each time I added a large slug of vodka to it.

I am not, nor am ever likely to be an expert on any particular method of losing weight. I am also fully aware that my weight loss regime would have horrified any professional exponent of the industry that has become *Health and Fitness*. My regime suited me well enough at the time, though, and had the added bonus of ensuring that I wore a permanent smile on my face pretty much from just after breakfast until supper.

As the pounds began to melt away, the next step towards making myself presentable enough to join a dating site was the acquisition of a new wardrobe, a prospect which both excited and terrified me in equal measure. As a thin person who had been trapped inside the body of both halves of the *Two Fat Ladies* for an over-sized portion of her life, the changing rooms in clothes stores were not something I chose to subject myself to. I preferred instead, to order my clothes online and try them on in the discomfort of my own home. The downside to this was that, despite paying a premium for plus-sized garments, those that populated my wardrobe were generally devoid of any style or elegance.

I discovered that a welcome bi-product of weight loss was an increase in my levels of confidence. These improved to such an extent that I felt the time had come for me to face up to my nemesis and visit a well-known department store in search of some new clothes. I was hoping to find something that not only catered for my wobbly bits but came in a choice of designs that didn't look like a camping accessory, just in three different colours.

I arrived at my chosen store feeling distinctly out of place in the context of the glitz and glamour of the beautifully lit space on the ground level. It had been a long time since I had cause to peruse the array of cosmetic and jewellery counters typical of stores such as these, having usually relied on my local supermarket for such items instead. I averted my gaze away from the staff standing beside the displays of perfume, all of whom looked like clones of airline cabin crew.

I sauntered around trying to assume the air of a regular customer at the same time as trying to figure out where I would find the ladieswear department and more specifically the portion of it reserved for larger sizes. Trying to promote this air of nonchalance, I picked up a bottle of perfume and began to spray it liberally around my neck and wrist areas. This had the immediate effect of alerting a member of the cabin crew, who I had previously presumed was a manikin, to my presence. With a bemused expression on her face, she handed me several testing strips which, because of my lack of familiarity with the whole testing protocol, had completely escaped my notice. In an effort to hide my embarrassment at this omission, I immediately changed my expression to one that suggested that the smell now engulfing us both, was not dissimilar to the odour emitted by a pile of fresh dog shit. The manikin responded sweetly by saying that she had never seen a reaction quite like mine before to Chanel No5.

Despite appearances to the contrary, the manikin then took me completely by surprise and with all the strength of a Russian shot-putter, guided me towards something resembling a bar stool for the purposes of a free make-over. Given that I suffer from vertigo when asked to climb anything higher than your average doorstep, I was particularly alarmed to then be raised off the ground to a height where an unaided escape was no longer possible. As I dangled helplessly in mid-air the manikin began her professional appraisal of my *vintage* approach to makeup, with particular reference to my lack of any discernible eyebrow line. She then proceeded to recommend products aimed at delivering a more on-trend look, the cost of which would have given a Drag Queen cause to reassess his/her career options. The advantages of supermarket and mail-order shopping had never been more apparent to me as I managed to locate the lever at the side of the bar stool which allowed me to re-enter Earth's atmosphere. I politely thanked the manikin for her unsolicited advice and added that I had noted her comments concerning the sparsity of my eyebrows. After due consideration, however, I had decided that I had no desire to replicate her undoubtedly on-trend look, but which seemed to me to be uncannily reminiscent of two marauding caterpillars at a melee.

When I finally located the ladieswear department, I set about selecting dresses, suits and shoes that I hoped would help me to appear more fanciable on a dating site before taking a deep breath and heading for the changing rooms. I was nervous that, despite the reduction in my size, the assistance of the in-store maintenance team might still be necessary in order for me to leave it without the narrow changing cubicle still clinging to my hips. Thanks to the effects of my *Lovely Latte* and vodka-infused shakes I left the store completely of my own volition armed with a selection of garments that were sufficiently flattering to further inflate my levels of confidence. This was undoubtedly a thrilling moment in my metamorphosis and another consultation with my *Mirror Mirror on the wall* this time confirmed that, whilst there was still room for improvement, there was no reason for me to delay my research into internet dating sites any longer.

Some Day My Prince Will Come?

Although I was disinclined to admit to it at the time, somewhere in the darkest recesses of my mind a fleeting thought was starting to take hold. Whilst my motivation for exploring the methods used by the *Catfishers* remained my primary motivation, I started to ponder on what might happen if I were to encounter a person who interested me on a personal level. Prior to this, the mere thought of another relationship was abhorrent to me. The very notion was usually quickly wrapped up in a parcel of guilt and sent packing post haste, but for some reason, it was now being returned to sender on an increasingly regular basis.

These questions concerning the possibility of a new and different friendship/relationship for myself became more persistent despite the more unpalatable aspects of what this might mean in practise. For instance, there was the not-insignificant question of sex within the context of a new relationship. The intimate chemistry that had existed between myself and Kenny right up until the later stages of his life, was not something I expected I would be fortunate enough to experience again. However, there is no denying that sex is an important part of any relationship that outsteps the boundaries of mere companionship. Therefore, the resumption of some kind of sex life, or at least one that didn't rely on an item powered by two double A batteries was a necessary consideration. If this slightly shifting pattern in the shape of my grieving was difficult to articulate even to myself, then it was practically impossible to do so elsewhere.

The words sex and widowhood are, quite frankly, mutually incompatible. Celibacy seems to be a requirement that is hard-wired into the terms and conditions of a widow's job specification. My marriage ended only as a result of the death of my husband and there were still those among my family and friends who expected me to cleave to the vows I made in 1978, despite the inclusion of the words *Till death us do part.* Those who conduct affairs within their marriages or who dissolve their obligations to marriage by choice, receive no particular attention when they decide to move on and nor should it attract any. There is no such tolerance, however, when it comes to a widow who wants to do the same thing.

Casting off a widow's weeds is an uncomfortable process for all those except the person unfortunate enough to have reason to wear them in the first place. As we start to dispense with the uniform of grief, we become less identifiable and far more unpredictable. As a consequence, we are also far more awkward to deal with. Researching dating sites as a source of material for my books was completely accepted by those in my inner circle right up until the point when I articulated that I was becoming increasingly receptive to the idea of merging my 42DD assets with someone who might be interested in making such an investment. The outraged response was such that you would have thought that I had suggested taking on the whole of the local rugby team on the try line. It was also assumed that by announcing myself as a solvent widow on a dating site I would only attract the scammers I sought to expose and nobody worthy of consideration in any serious sense. It was evident to me that there was a much greater emphasis placed on the protection of my fiscal well-being than either my emotional or mental health equivalent.

I spent a minimal amount of time weighing up the opinions of all those who presumed to know more about walking in my shoes than I did. They had not experienced the pain of fitting feet into new shoes which insisted they walked to places they didn't want to go, so I simply ignored them. The facts were straightforward enough-the majority of sand in my egg timer was already in the bottom half of it and my losses were already quantified in a way that any future gains were not. On this basis, I figured that teaching my shoes how to walk towards places of my choosing, even if this was without the approval of others, was a worthy pursuit.

Chapter 2

Fail To Prepare-Prepare To Fail

Stuff Worth Remembering

At this point in the proceedings, I make no apologies for repeating information that is included in my first book **The Funny Thing About Being a Widow?** The following updated extracts contain important safety information for readers who have come straight to this, the second book in the series, and will, therefore, have missed it. Even with those of you already acquainted with the following, a reminder of the dos and don'ts is unlikely to be disadvantageous, but feel free to proceed to the next chapter if you would prefer.

Safety First

Some of the practices that should help to preserve our safety when using dating sites, might seem, at face value, to be nothing more than basic common sense. Despite knowing all that I am about to impart prior to my excursion into the world of online dating, I readily admit to ignoring most of my own advice. Common sense is an acuity that is easily overridden by complacency and a false sense of impunity. Thankfully, more by good luck than good judgment, I escaped from any disastrous consequences of my, at times, blasé attitude towards internet safety.

Be In The Right Place At The Right Time

The internet is reflective of society in general, in that it plays host to an eclectic array of tastes, beliefs and lifestyle choices. It should go without saying that unless you have a particular penchant for facial hair, for example, a site that offers suitors of an exclusively hirsute nature, is unlikely to yield the results you are looking for if you do not. My research uncovered the existence of dating sites that catered for married people who were looking for no-strings-attached extracurricular adventures. Others I found restricted their membership to those who were morbidly obese, as well as various fetish sites and even one at the time of writing somewhat inexplicably catering specifically for those who eat salad. It is, therefore, safe to say that the importance of carefully matching your expectations against what is offered by any site you choose cannot be overstated.

It is also worthy of note that sites which appear to have no obvious relationship, can and do share profile information between them. It was not uncommon for me to go on a date with someone who assumed that I had subscribed to the same site as they had, but our profiles had been shared in different places which had different titles.

To Pay Or Not To Pay

There are many free dating sites out there to choose from, but because they do not require a monetary investment it can mean that those using them might not be looking for serious, or long-term, relationships. It does not necessarily follow, that by paying to use the services of a dating site, you are more likely to connect with a genuine prospect, but it does at least imply that some level of effort has been made. The paid-for sites usually benefit from a degree of moderation too, though the effectiveness of this can vary greatly. Some sites will allow you to join initially for free and will let you add a profile including pictures to gauge the level and type of response you can expect to receive. However, you are not allowed to communicate with any interested party until you commit to a fully paid-up subscription to the site.

Since my foray into internet dating, the apps we can now download to our phones have revolutionised even this relatively new way of seeking out people to date and have a relationship with. When referring to dating apps in this context, I use the word date in its broadest sense because some of these types of apps serve to facilitate nothing more than a casual hook-up. The more well-known dating apps tend to be frequented by an age group which would have excluded me on that basis alone, and I admit that the culture of swiping left or right is not one I find to be particularly attractive.

Stay On The Site

My intention to attract the attention of *Catfishers,* and other romance fraudsters was accomplished to a greater or lesser degree on each of the four sites I used for my research. Some of these people are easily identifiable, as in when the fraudsters use the profile picture of a wealthy celebrity, whom we might reasonably assume, does not need the services of a dating site. Of course, there are other far more sophisticated scams out there too, which makes the golden rule of communicating within the limits of your chosen site even more important, especially at the start of any communication.

You will find that romance fraudsters often prefer more immediate and direct forms of communication. Commensurate with achieving this aim, they may ask you to talk to them on other platforms such as your personal email account or WhatsApp. It is always inadvisable to acquiesce to requests for more detailed personal information, even that of a surname until you are confident that the person you are talking to, is at least who they say they are.

Google 'em!

After Kenny died, I felt I had no choice but to engage with the world outside of the one we created and happily resided within for most of our adult lives. I was aware of the existence of something called the World Wide Web but viewed it with the same level of scepticism I used to reserve for microwaves when they first came onto the scene. To me the internet seemed overly complicated to use, largely unnecessary and potentially harmful.

These days, of course, it is practically impossible to survive in the modern age in which we live without the internet and all the rapidly evolving technology associated with it. With little consideration of the implications of doing so, we happily surrender the management of our whole lives to this entity, entrusting it with all manner of personal information ranging from the minutiae of our financial arrangements, to that offered up to the public via social media accounts. Whilst this ease of access to information can leave us vulnerable to exploitation, the flip side of this is that the information provided by Google can also be a useful tool to help confirm or refute any details given to you by a prospective date. The trick is to extrapolate the information that is useful to you whilst ignoring that which serves no purpose, whilst also remembering that not everything you read online is an accurate representation of the truth.

One lady I talked to discovered that a man she had plans to meet with had several tattoos after she checked out his profile on FaceBook. This was something he had gone to great lengths to hide in his pictures on the dating site. I did not agree, however, with her conclusion that this discovery might mean that he was a hardened criminal, although it did point towards a lack of candour, which is never a good sign.

Meeting and Greeting

When, and if, this stage is reached and an actual date is arranged, basic precautions are common sense. Never allow someone you have never met to pick you up from your home address for a first date. I was guilty of a blatant breach of this most obvious of safety rules as you will read about later on in this book.

Arrange to meet in a place where there are lots of other people around and get someone to call you about half an hour into the date to check that you are safe and to give you an excuse to fake some kind of emergency if you feel the need to bail. It is not a good idea either to agree to get into the car of someone you have met in this way on the premise of changing the venue of the date to somewhere other than that arranged.

Food and Drink

Dating for the first time after a long marriage or partnership can illicit a heady mix of emotions and sometimes, as a result of this, we can neglect to be as vigilant as we might otherwise be. Drinking too much is never a good idea on a first date, although I missed that particular memo too, because we might be less aware of the possibility of noxious substances being added to food or drink. Thankfully, date rape is relatively rare amongst internet daters in middle age, but it can and does happen. It is always good practice to be aware of this whilst eating and drinking with a stranger.

Categories

I am the first to admit that my organisational skills are right up there with those of a three-year-old. So, in an attempt to redress this issue, I have created the five categories that follow to help define the most common characteristics I encountered in men frequenting the dating sites I researched for ease of reference.

The Scammers

A group of men who are comprised entirely of those intent on gaining a financial or emotional advantage. They are often not who they purport to be and their skills of deception vary from laughable to those that are of a very sophisticated level. They are commonly referred to as *Catfishers* and more details of my experiences with members of this group follow in later chapters of this book.

The Barely Breathers

This category consists of very elderly men whose demise is likely imminent, or judging by the images I encountered in some of their profile pictures might have already occurred. Some of the men in this group are clearly in pursuit of a carer-with-benefits type of arrangement. An example of this was when I was asked by one game-old geezer if I would have any objection to him eating his fried eggs directly from my breasts. I replied that only if he liked ostrich eggs as a regular-sized hen job would not provide the necessary coverage.

Not all of the messages I receive from men in this category are of this ilk. Some of them were just lonely and content to have an opportunity to chat with a woman such as Fred who is eighty-one years old. When, during one of our online conversations I complained that I was beginning to despair of ever finding a man suitable enough to date he sent me the following message in response.

No, darling, maps and compasses are of no use to you on this site. What you would find useful though is a good prat nav because anyone who cannot see the kind soul lurking behind that beautiful face of yours deserves to show up on your screen so that you can steer well clear of them. Take very good care of yourself and stay safe.

The Perverts

Although there are some of these in the preceding category, I reserve this particular heading for the more sinister type of pervert who deserve a classification of their own. The perverts can be difficult to spot initially. Their early messages often give nothing away that will alert you to their true agenda and they can be quite skilled in gaining your trust so that they can move you away from the site.

Once they achieve this, however, their messages start to assume a more sexually explicit tone. At one stage, I amassed a collection of phallic examples in the gallery of my phone which ranged in size from that of a foot-long sub to that of a glue stick.

The Serial Winkers

Winking in dating site terms is a way in which you can alert someone to your interest without going to the bother of sending a message. This group is an interesting one in that its members appear to be decent enough guys who do not show any of the tendencies or behaviours which would earn them admission to the group reserved for perverts.

One of the sites I was a member of had a dating diary facility and the following is an entry I submitted which, in my view, sums up the members of this category perfectly.

I do not like the term winking even if I understand that here in the world of online dating, it is used to expedite communications between members. What I don't understand are the serial winkers who do so several times a day on most days of the week. When you add this up over a month it starts to amount to a seriously exhausting amount of winking. On the occasions that I have tried to respond to this type of winker with a message, it often goes ignored whilst the winker in question continues to wink away at a furious pace. I can only assume that winkers who do this are sufficiently satisfied by the act of winking alone, that they have no actual need to proceed further than a wink.

The Ifs, Buts & Maybes

This category is by far the one containing the smallest number of members. Those that do make it into this category, are regarded to be worthy of further investigation.

I include the results of some of these investigations in later chapters of this book.

Chapter 3

A Brave New World

To The Profile and Beyond

Creating a profile for a dating site can most definitely lead us into temptation. It is, after all, an opportunity to present ourselves exactly as we would wish to be perceived, and this can lead to a tendency to overindulge our creative sides to the detriment of our credibility. I had lost quite a lot of weight prior to creating my profile, but I still had a fair way to go before I achieved a BMI that fell within the acceptable range. So, I ensured that any photographs included in my profile were taken from a flattering angle that focused on my face and away from anything below the neck. I stopped short of using filters, not just because my ignorance of technology would not allow it, but because you can only stretch the truth so far before it snaps completely.

Instead, I concentrated on creating a pitch designed to be intriguing and of course, of sufficient interest to attract the *Catfishers* I was hoping to ensnare in my keep net. For those of you not as keen to find rotten fish on the end of their lines, my best advice when it comes to creating a profile is to keep it as simple and honest as you can without giving any clues as to your location or full identity.

The Dating Sites- An Overview

In the process of trying to make useful comparisons between sites, in terms of the services and features they offered, I decided to enrol with four well-known brands. I paid a fee to join each site but found no discernible advantage in the quality of the experience of the more expensive sites when compared to those whose fees were considerably lower.

I haven't included any information concerning some of the dating apps that have exploded onto the scene since I conducted my research because (a) my lack of technical know-how was, not for the first time, a barrier to my understanding of how they worked and (b) they were also pitched towards younger age groups, though now there are some which cater for a more mature clientele. However, the principles of safety and vigilance, remain the same for the users of all types of online dating.

Despite having studied the pros and cons of each site that I joined, I am not able to provide any definitive recommendations as to which ones are likely to work best. I realise that for those of you who came to this book in the hope of finding such recommendations, this might be something of a disappointment. However, for me to suggest that any one site will deliver successful outcomes for all those that join them, would be akin to suggesting that larger ladies have any chance whatsoever of fitting into a pair of one-size tights. It is also worth bearing in mind that the primary purpose of my research was to expose the methods used by *Catfishers.* Therefore, the definition of a site's success from my perspective will not only be different from yours but, when defined in this way, possibly quite unhelpful as a result. Ultimately, choosing a dating site has much in common with the lottery in that you pay your money, make your choice and you will either win or you won't. What I hope you will take from the following, is information that helps you to refine your search to at least the type of site that you think might best meet your needs.

A Degree In Science - Site Number 1

This site was the most expensive of all those I trialled and represented a not insignificant investment. I was required to complete an extensive questionnaire at the outset, which for someone like me whose boredom threshold is abnormally low was a distinct and early disadvantage. This detailed information was then fed into the system's algorithms which use it to make suggestions as to who your best potential matches might be based on similarities in interests, lifestyle choices and attitudes.

This slightly pseudo-scientific approach may seem on the face of it to be an eminently sensible one, though it appeared to me to have some fairly fundamental drawbacks. Any matches between opposites, for example, will fall outside the criteria that the algorithms are designed to pair up, precisely because of those differences. Whilst the chances of finding much common ground between a stamp collector and a pole dancer, for instance, is likely to be low statistically, it is not altogether impossible. If algorithms can identify recurring patterns and match them accordingly, they cannot know if the information on which they base their predictions is authentic in the first place. This a system that is heavily reliant on the integrity of those who use it and who are free to manipulate it in whatever way they choose.

After the considerable effort of completing what at times felt like a university entrance exam, I was hugely disappointed by the low level of matches I received once I had. I fully expected that my status as a widow alone would guide at least some *Catfishers* toward the bait wriggling on the end of my hook, but they were few in number on this site, preferring to swim together in much larger shoals elsewhere.

I concluded, that the cost of this site was probably a prohibitive factor for a fraudster who could just as easily ply his stock in trade on sites which were cheaper or even free. The avoidance of this unnecessarily high business expense was likely to be far more cost-effective for them in the long run.

The few matches that were suggested for me on this site, were all successful professional men. Behind this elevated status, though, I unearthed the existence of some fairly stereotypical ideas concerning widows who frequent this genre of dating site. Despite including brief details of my past endeavours, which included being a former Company Director, it was my status as a widow that prompted any discussions initiated by men on this site.

One chap, in particular, contacted me on account of my *gorgeous profile pictures* but also commented that, despite being drawn to them, he was very wary of my status as a widow. Despite his admission that he had never even spoken to a widow on the site before, let alone dated someone who had lost their husband, his fear was that he might forever be held up in comparison to a dead spouse. I have some understanding of why this might be a particular concern, although personally speaking I have never sought to compare the incomparable, preferring to respond to people according to who they are rather than what I would like them to be.

Another of his concerns was the possibility that a widowed lady might have a specific financial agenda now that they no longer enjoyed the support of a husband. Again, I suppose this could be true of some widowed ladies, or gentlemen for that matter, but I had hoped that my profile indicated that this was probably not my reason for being on a dating site. I think I was more irked by the fact that this guy focused solely on my status as a widow and very little else. I consoled myself by filling my face with a cream cake in celebration of the slight manipulations that I had been guilty of during the production of the aforementioned *gorgeous profile pictures.* Quite why this man's concerns for his future fiscal well-being were concentrated on the possible motives of a bereaved woman as opposed to one who might be skint as the result of an acrimonious divorce, was as baffling as it is, unfortunately, typical.

In summary, I found this site to be overly complicated and felt that it did not represent good value for money. It did not generate any matches that came close to anything that might lead to a date. The lack of scammers on this site, whilst a definite plus for anyone whose purpose was not to research their methods, was a disappointment for someone with my agenda. Had I been just a regular punter looking to find a meaningful relationship through the medium of online dating and this site had been my first port of call, I may well have abandoned any further efforts beyond this point.

Birds Of A Feather Flock Together - Site Number 2

Site number two was one whose membership was comprised solely of widows and widowers and I expected this site would be heavily populated by *Catfishers* and other romance fraudsters. Another reason for joining this one was to see if being amongst a collective of people who had a shared experience in common might make the establishment of new friendships or relationships easier. I discovered that, whilst sharing empathy in this way was an advantage, there were also some downsides associated with it. Having lived through my own experience of loss and reaching a place where my focus had shifted towards the future, I found that there was a tendency amongst members to dwell on where we had come from as opposed to where we might be heading.

This site was well-moderated, which was a definite positive when it comes to a place used by vulnerable people, and as a result was not a place where *Catfishers* were able to act with the impunity I had expected. Other plus points include that it was reasonably priced and easy to join and use. The main disadvantage of this site was that overall membership numbers were low, which in the context of meeting the criteria for joining it, might be construed as a good thing, though not necessarily when it comes to looking for a new relationship/date. Within this number, there was also a much higher ratio of women to men. This is also very common on other forums available for bereaved spouses but again creates a disparity on a site aimed at facilitating dates between members of the opposing sex.

Overall, my experience here was underwhelming, rather than overtly positive or negative. It did generate a lead for a date, though, the details of which I include in a later chapter.

Seek and You Shall Find - Site Number 3

The third of the four sites was a paid-for version of a very popular free dating site. As I have said, both in my previous book and then again here, I do think that a paid investment helps to demonstrate a degree of effort. Conversely, this was also the site where I discovered the highest number of fake profiles and romance scammers. It is worth noting, however, that it was a broad umbrella which included profiles that had originated on other similar sites with the resultant effect of a much larger number of users when compared to that of the other sites I looked at. The category I created for those deserving of the title of pervert, was also heavily represented with members from this, and its partner sites.

The title I selected was age-specific and pitched at those who were in the middle age bracket and upwards, however, this did not stop much younger people of both sexes from accessing the site and not because they were looking for a grandparent to adopt. It was Mrs Merton, the alter ego of the late great Caroline Aherne, who once asked Debbie Magee what it was that had first attracted her to her *millionaire* husband, the magician Paul Daniels, who is also sadly no longer with us. Though this particular union was undoubtedly a loving and durable one, the cynicism implicit in Mrs Merton's question is worth remembering on a dating site frequented by young pretenders. Again, my own experience in this regard is included in the following pages.

Not one to shy away from writing about my experiences, I made full use of the opportunity to record them on the *dating diary* facility offered on this site. I found that this helped me to make more connections than I might have otherwise. It was also this site that taught me everything I would ever need to know about all the things I didn't want in my life after losing Kenny. The depth of my gratitude concerning this, however, pales into insignificance beside the good fortune of finding my current husband under a quirky black hat which he used in his profile picture and which prompted the first of our messages.

In summary, this site delivered on all levels. I found examples of everything I had been seeking and some that I had not been expecting. It was also simple to use and affordable, proving in my case to be well worth the modest investment.

My experiences with the people I met on this site comprise the majority of the content in this book. Whilst I hope you are entertained by reading about them, if they also serve to impart valuable lessons that I was much too slow to learn then I consider this to be a job well done.

Last and Least - Site Number 4

This was another well-recognised brand name and I am personally aware of people for whom it worked well and led to the establishment of several wonderful relationships.

Not unlike site number one it too requests quite a lot of personal information to match you to suitable prospects. Of course, also like site number one, the validity of these matches is only as good as the integrity of the information on which they are based. Thankfully, though, the questionnaire on this site was not nearly as lengthy or mind-numbing as the first, a distinct advantage to someone like me who is well known for having an attention span consistent with that of an amoeba.

I was offered a decent number of suggested suitors here, but I could not progress any of the subsequent conversations to the point where either party was willing to put in the effort required to meet in person. I struggled to understand why this site didn't seem to work for me but concluded that because site number three was already my firm favourite, I probably didn't try as hard as I might have to fully exploit the potential of this one.

In summary, this site was at the higher end of the scale of expense but was more straightforward to use than others of a similar cost and type. Having personal knowledge of several success stories made me consider that this was a site that might work well for those more willing to spend time exploiting its features than I was.

Chapter 4

Gone Fishing

Catching A Live One

Once my hips had reduced sufficiently in size, I enrolled in each of the aforementioned dating sites and prepared to whip out my bait and tackle at long last.

I had no idea what to expect beyond this point, but began my explorations with an open mind, a degree of trepidation and I would be lying if I didn't admit to a degree of excitement too.

Red Flags & Alarm Bells

The experience of seeing the faces of strange men scroll across the bottom of the screen on my laptop was a little unnerving at first. A good majority of these pictures looked as though they had been taken for either passport purposes or for that of a police station mugshot. Reverse image apps, if they existed at all back then, would not have been on my radar such was my ignorance of the workings of social media and the internet in general. Nowadays, I use them regularly to help me identify the fake profiles that still plague me on a daily basis across all of my social media accounts.

I would spend an inordinate amount of time studying these images. I scrutinised every detail including what I could make out in the background too, searching for anything inconsistent with the information in someone's profile information. Sometimes a car number plate or a road sign would indicate that the actual location of a photograph was different to where the person in it was claiming to be at the time. I conducted a similarly forensic dissection of the written profiles before I would send a standard speculative message to those men I suspected would be the most likely to take my bait. I have included unaltered examples of some of the responses I received below, all of which qualified them for admission to my category of perverts.

Me: *Hi I'm Sandra I read your profile and think that we might have a lot in common. I would love to hear back from you if you thought so too.*

Gordon: *So glad you came calling sexy lady I would love to get to know you better I have to warn you though that I have a very very sexy eye.*

Me: *Really? That must irritate the hell out of the other one. Hope you get them both to work together eventually. Thanks for stopping by.*

Trevor: *Hello Sandra I have read your profile and agree that we would get along great especially if you got your tits out. I wouldn't be able to stop whistling at them.*

Me: *Well, hello there Mr Charisma. At my age, I have to inform you my tits are not the perky puppies they once were and no matter how long or hard you whistle at them, they won't be bounding towards you with their tongues hanging* *out anytime soon. Hope those dentures you borrowed from Mister Ed are glued in tight though, you don't want them to go west when you're whistling.*

Robert: *I love that pic of you wearing a white and brown top. I think I can see your nipple poking out and that makes me think you might like some big fat cock action. Come fly with me if you want to ride on my skyrocket made for two.*

Me: *Hello Robert. I am glad you liked my top and for all I know there may well be yet-to-be-discovered tribes of women out there in the universe who do indeed have multiple* nipples. Fortunately, I *do not and if you can't tell the difference between a printed polka dot on my top and a woman's nipple, I am forced to conclude that your skyrocket is probably not big enough for anything other than solo journeys either.*

Harold: *Hey big tits how are you doing today?*

I am no prude, but the rest of this delightful message sent to me by a gross individual called Harold and was so graphically explicit that I elected not to include the rest of it here in the interests of taste and decency. I did alert the moderators of the site from which it originated to the obscene nature of its content and they responded appropriately by removing Harold from the site. Purely for my own entertainment purposes, I fired off the following missive first. Harold was indeed a worthy recipient of an award I reserved for the worst of all those who qualified for a place in my category reserved for perverts.

Me: *My goodness Harold what a tall tale you tell! Here is one I wrote in response which is nowhere near as fictional as it might at first appear to be.*

How Truncheon Meat Was Invented

By Sandra E Manning

Living a miserable existence in a dingy little hovel, there once lived a quite revolting old curmudgeon who, because of his repulsive features, obnoxious behaviours, and total lack of personality had no friends at all. So, this nasty old specimen, whose own mother even refused to touch him without the protection of a full Hazmat suit, spent all his time prodding the keys on his laptop with podgy, dirty little digits to write grotesque messages that he would send to women who would have never risked their eyesight to look at him once, never mind twice.

One particular evening, he made a fatal error by sending a very sexually explicit message to a lady in the next village. As he intended it would, the act of doing so got him overly excited but this time he wasn't able to grab a tissue from the pocket-sized pack that was permanently by his side and the only other participant in his sordid sex life. Unfortunately, this miscalculation meant that his laptop acquired a very sticky E as a permanent consequence.

The lady who received the message was disgusted by its content but knew that it could only have been sent by a sexually inadequate individual who would not have been able to garner her attention in any other way. This lady was very smart though, and used her skills as a writer to cleverly edit the foul message. She then posted the results, along with a picture of the original author, to whom she gave full accreditation, on the noticeboard in her village of Spacenook.

Before she knew it the post went on to cause something called a virus which quickly spread all around not just her village, but to others far and wide.

Usually, I write happy endings for my stories Harold, but I suspect you are beyond redemption and are unlikely to benefit from the same type of intervention which saved another miserable old bastard created by Charles Dickens from eternal damnation. I have, however, arranged for you to receive a visitation of a different and more tangible nature.

So, Harold now might be a good time to pop your tiny little Weiner sausage back inside your pants before the arrival of a PC Pounder who is on his way to escort you around to his place after tracing something called your IP address. If you are quick maybe you will manage to do this before he whips out his truncheon and uses it to tenderise your pathetic little penis with it first. Truncheon meat...now that Just might catch on!

The Language of Love

As I began to spend more time on dating sites it wasn't long before the *Catfishers and romance fraudsters* who were motivated more by financial gratification rather than anything sexual started to swim to the surface to take the bait. Their responses to my speculative message contained many examples of the following red flags that should always serve to ring alarm bells. A high proportion of romance fraudsters operate out of countries in West Africa, so English is not their first language and as a consequence, they tend to pluralise words inappropriately which is a fairly easy spot. Sometimes when I challenged these and other lapses in the appropriate use of English, the fraudster would claim to originate from a country in Europe and be studying English.

God's Will

A message that is littered with religious references can be another indication that it comes from a scammer. The inclusion of phrases that constantly refer to *God's will* or someone who describes themselves as *God-fearing* or *blessed* can also be big clues. Of course, not all people of faith who use terminology such as this are disingenuous, but it is a feature that cropped up regularly in my conversations with those who were subsequently found to be less than genuine.

Teamwork

Scammers do not always work alone. They can be part of teams and, when organised properly, this practice can be quite difficult to spot. In examples of this type, the scammer is not just one person but several who work in shifts. In one long-running series of WhatsApp messages that I was involved in before he/they made an error, the messages had seemed authentic, and until this point I had assumed them to be part of a genuine communication. Shift patterns are easier to detect when the gangs operating them are sloppy and do not properly account for differences in time zones or check the details and progress of their narrative before a handover.

The Funny Thing About A Scam

The understanding of humour is another area where certain nuances and points of cultural reference do not always translate very well. The scammers tend to ignore what they haven't understood, and when they do make an attempt to engage with something that is obviously said in jest, they do so in ways that are not always relevant.

It is worth noting that these fraudsters also operate outside of traditional dating sites. The conversation which follows, took place with a guy who contacted me after we had played online Scrabble, which, unsurprisingly, I won with a minimum of effort given his tenuous grasp of the English language.

In this example, I was deliberate in my use of references that people outside of my own age group might struggle to understand to help illustrate the above points concerning cultural reference and humour. Whilst it is clear that this was a communication forged out of a fraudulent intention, not all examples are as blatantly as obvious as this one. This guy claimed to be from England and we conducted the following conversation on Messenger after he found me on Facebook. This exchange took place over a few days with gaps in between responses, which was probably due to the differences in our time zones and shift changes. Again, I have left the spelling and punctuation in these messages exactly as they were when I received them.

Catfisher: *Hello beautiful how are you doing today? I hope you are great I'm sorry for adding you up but your profile made me not hang back and want to add you up. I want us to know more about each other if you have a mind. Where are you from please?*

Me: *I am from a place called Gilligan's Island and am just on a boat called the SS Minnow at the present time.*

Scammer: *Oh that's nice. So if you leave there where will you go are you happily married with kids?*

Me: *After my boat trip is over, I am going to take another trip this time on a train with a guy called Casey Jones. Unfortunately, I am not happily married, but I have two lovely kids called Bart and Lisa.*

Scammer: *Oh that is nice. Well I am sorry you are not happy with your husband but God knows best and have better plans. Who is Casey Jones? I am a single dad of a beautiful daughter I cherish so much I lost my wife by some gun men who shot her dead while coming back from work.*

Me: *Casey is the train driver and we will be a steaming and a rolling quite soon. I am even hoping that he will sign his cap for me. I am sorry to hear about the death of your wife that must have been awful for you.*

Scammer: *I was emotionally devastated but I have to stay strong for my kid and give her the best life. I appreciate you I hope you don't mind your email and phone number?*

Me: *No, I don't mind them at all, I find both quite useful actually.*

Scammer: *You didn't send me your number I am looking for a sole mate and want to know you better.*

Me: *Really? Do you like Sole? I prefer Catfish personally. Sorry about the number I have a memory like a goldfish. How's your son doing? He must miss his mother terribly.*

Scammer: *Not so good my dear he needs to have a kidney transplant. But no money to complete the payment and I might lose him.*

Me: *Oh my goodness, things must be bad your son was your daughter only a few texts ago. Those dodgy kidneys can really mess you up, can't they?*

The next message I received was a picture of a mobile phone whose screen had been smashed to the extent that it was probably not usable.

Scammer: *My phone makes me press the wrong words I have a daughter Alondra and she is dying. I just need $2,500 to complete the treatment that is all I need my dear. I feel like hanging myself to death.*

Me: *Oh, don't do that you might just break your neck and then you would need money for a wheelchair as well. Does your English doctor charge you in dollars? It is quite cheap though for a kidney. Are you getting a buy one get one free deal?*

Scammer: *Can you lend me the money or not my kid will die without treatment I will pay you back with interest.*

Me: *Well, I do have a spare £20,000 in my piggy bank if that would help?*

Scammer: *How Can you get it for me I will be very grateful if you can help save my son*

Me: *Your daughter is a boy again now?*

Scammer: *no she is a girl but her nanny is a boy.*

At this point, I received a picture of a middle-aged blonde woman lying on a hospital gurney surrounded by doctors marking her up for something that looked like a cosmetic procedure.

Me: *Crikey! Alondra has had it rough she looks even older than me!*

Scammer: *Cant you understand my little girl is dying and the doctors need money first before they will complete the treatment Can you buy Bitcoins with your piggy bank?*

Me: *Nope I only have pound notes.*

Scammer: *Just hold and I will send you bank details to transfer the money send me a screenshot when you are done ok?*

The bank details provided were traced back to a Bank of America account on Broadway in New York and were subsequently passed on to the relevant authorities. No further action was taken because I had not suffered any losses and the people who perpetrate these scams are also very skilled when it comes to covering their tracks, making the pursuit of them time-consuming and expensive.

I did send a screenshot as requested, but it was a photograph of my beautiful pink piggy bank which I would like to reassure everyone suffered no adverse effects as a result of its involvement with my undercover sting.

Competition Fraud

We are all familiar with the messages that take up an annoying amount of space in our Spam emails, telling us that we have won a competition that we know we haven't even entered. This form of scam is growing rapidly in popularity amongst online fraudsters and I have decided to include the following example because of its parallels with the communications used by the romance fraudsters. It is also interesting to see how this scammer weaves in some checkable facts to help give their pitch more credibility.

This particular scam is based on something similar to the postcode lottery that we have in the UK. The scammer who contacted me through one of my social media accounts claimed to be a representative of a genuine US-based company that also presents cheques to winners on their doorsteps.

The image used by the scammer was of someone who was a legitimate associate of the company and would have been unaware of the fact that their photo was being used in this scam. I have left all the messages in the form that they were sent and received.

Me: *Hello do you have an enquiry I can help you with?*

Scammer: *My name is* (genuine name of company associate) *as you can see from my profile it is really nice to meet you*

Me: *Likewise. Yes, I have read your profile where you say that you are the claim agent for ******** which is very reassuring as I wouldn't want to be talking to a fake one! What can I do for you?*

Scammer: *I am the real one okay? I'm your friend in delight to be and I have been authorised to tell you on behalf of our CEO* (genuine name) *that you are our latest grand prize winner.*

Me: *I won an actual prize? What on earth did I do? I can't usually win an argument in an empty room so I am very excited.*

Scammer: *Well congratulations! You have been randomly selected to receive our grand prize of $1 Million and an extra $7,000 weekly for life courtesy of ******* All set to be delivered within 48 hours by me at your home no later than 3 o'clock noon tomorrow and yes this is no game or gimmicks as we are a company that only seek to help people Okay so congratulations.*

Cue some pictures of previous winners receiving their doorstep cheques in pictures taken from the internet.

Me: *Seriously? You are coming to my home tomorrow at 3.00pm noon? I mean that hardly gives me enough time to sweep up let alone bake a cake! What's your favourite? I like carrot cake can I dangle one of those in front of you? I can't breathe with excitement!*

Scammer: *We are all set but I just need some information from you. Full name, home address, phone number and email address.*

Me: *OK no problem can I just ask you though how you will get from New York to Bognor Regis by 3.00pm noon tomorrow? I thought travelling was restricted because of the pandemic.*

Scammer: *We are allowed because we have a signed contract with the government and the government is aware of this so there isn't a problem. I want you to get back to me so I can set things up we can also come today?*

Me: *OK but I won't be able to make the cake in time for today though.*

Scammer: *Don't worry about the cake. So fill in those informations so we could proceed on your winnings.*

Me: *Penelope Pitstop, 27 Silverstone Road, Brands Hatch, Bognor Regis. Zip: MUT Ley, Scotland UK. Professional writer, phone number 0800 12344321 email parker@pisstake.comic You sure about the cake?*

Scammer: *Okay good. Yes I am sure.*

Please note you are advised to keep the news of your winnings private and confidential. Do not tell any individual or group of people about your winnings due to security reasons that is someone else coming behind you to claim the winnings and it is against the law and policy guiding this lottery so adhere to it or violation of this policy will result in the cancellation of your winnings.

Me: *My lips are sealed I don't want to get violated.*

Scammer: *Okay good. Because your winnings is over $1 million by US law as our grand prize winner will have to get a US clearance receipt to show that you have registered and completed the 1% state to state tax charge which covers shipping and handling expense of your winnings. The payment of $250 can be made via any local store outlet and will be paid to a merchant banker whose information will be provided to you for completion. And immediately you make the payment your winnings would be delivered to you in no source of delay or difficulties. Okay I assure you.*

Needless to say, I did not pay $250, bake a bloody carrot cake or get a visit from anyone with a cheque for $1 million at 3.00pm noon.

Grooming

It might seem completely implausible that anyone would part with money when asked to do so in the aforementioned circumstances, but highly vulnerable people can be easily coerced. In 2020, romance fraud netted a staggering sum of sixty-three million pounds sterling in the UK alone and this is a figure set to rise even further. It is a highly lucrative industry and even scams that seem to be ridiculous will still be worth a punt for the *Catfisher* who works on an overall success rate percentage.

Love Bombing

The more sophisticated types of fraud, are often backed by organised crime, whose bigger resources take the art of scamming to a whole different level. However, common to all types of scams, is the existence of a vulnerability that the *Catfishers* are highly skilled in identifying and exploiting. During my time researching this subject, I discovered that former police officers, teachers and even a magistrate were amongst the victims who all lost substantial amounts to romance fraudsters. There is no such thing as a typical victim, just a lonely and vulnerable one.

A common technique used by a *Catfisher* is known as *love bombing*. The chosen target is subjected to a barrage of flattering messages during the very early days of any communication, and these should always be regarded as the huge red flag that they are. The compliments are commonly followed up by declarations of undying love and promises of future commitment.

Once I started to experience this for myself as a necessary part of my research, I was shocked to discover that I was nowhere near as indifferent towards its effects as I assumed I would be. I could see the red flags clearly enough and hear the alarm bells, but bizarrely, I was able to ignore both when it suited me. When you are subjected to this technique, usually in the relative safety of your own home, it is hard to see how indulging in a bit of harmless flattery could lead to a serious financial consequence. This is part of the *Catfisher's* game plan in that they use this feeling of impunity that comes from engaging with them in a non-threatening environment to their advantage. In my case, because I had lost a lot of weight and made several other positive changes to my appearance, I was already predisposed towards accepting the flattery levelled at me. It felt like a validation of those efforts, rather than the blanket *love bombing* technique that it actually was. With the benefit of hindsight, I came to appreciate just how little insight I had into the depths of my own vulnerability. Whilst this technique was ultimately unsuccessful in persuading me to part with any money, I did accept far too many deposits into my personal safety deposit box than was good for me, as I shall explain later.

The Inheritance or Asset Scam

Both of these scams are aimed at convincing the target that the fraudster has a significant investment in valuable commodities such as gold or diamonds, or that they have received a substantial inheritance. In either case, there are usually several barriers standing in the way of access to, and the conversion of these assets. One such example is the existence of a short-term cash flow problem, which means the fraudster is unable to fund export taxes or fees levied by governments. They may also say that because they are unable to pay for export licences to transport valuable goods, they have been arrested at the airport and need money to make bail.

The *Catfisher* might also offer what appear to be official documents to help validate their claims. A closer inspection will often reveal spelling errors or the inclusion of photoshopped images which would not be present in a genuine document. The quality of paperwork that is faked is largely dependent on the resources available to the fraudster producing them. Because of the highly effective grooming techniques used by the fraudsters, victims can be disinclined to inspect any paperwork provided to them beyond that which is cursory.

It is also quite common for other people to be introduced into the scam to help foster a sense of security in the victim. These are sometimes said to be family members of the fraudster or in other cases, they will be government officials in a bid to add another layer of authenticity to the scam in play.

When the grooming techniques employed by the fraudsters have been executed sufficiently well, the target at this stage, will believe that they are in a genuine and committed relationship. In these circumstances, most of us would be willing to help out a person we regard as a life partner and the victim is then persuaded to loan the money requested. The victim is also similarly convinced that any money lent is on the basis of a bona fide loan which will be repaid with interest once the fraudster's assets have been realised. They will probably have been further seduced by promises that the fraudster's assets will be of sufficiently high value to fund a comfortable lifestyle in the future.

These ploys are very typical examples of those that exist online. When it comes to actually meeting someone in the flesh, there are many additional trip hazards which need to be navigated, hopefully with more due diligence than I was capable of exercising at the time I encountered them.

Chapter 5

Pleased To Meet You?

Under Starter's Orders

I spent my first internet date hiding in a shed at my local garden centre, trying to avoid a man I had fully intended to meet. Given that this date was technically a non-starter, I probably shouldn't even mention it under this particular subheading. Anyone wishing to read about it can do so in my first book **The Funny Thing About Being a Widow?**

Despite this inauspicious start to my time on dating sites, I did go on to have quite a number of first dates, learning in the process that the simple act of turning up was conducive to meeting some genuinely nice men. The majority of the first dates that I have included in this chapter were not destined to be followed by another, for reasons that should be self-explanatory. Others did not progress beyond the scope of a nice couple of hours spent in polite conversation because it was obvious that no chemistry or common ground existed to justify it. One guy that I did have a few dates with was a lovely man who I still think about with fondness. During our brief time together, I think he was quite shocked to learn that he still had a lot of unresolved issues as a result of his relationship with his ex-wife. Because we realised that he perhaps wasn't as emotionally available as he genuinely believed himself to be, we decided not to pursue things any further than we may otherwise have. Despite an initial run of good luck, it wasn't long before I strayed into territory that suggested that my good fortune was about to exceed its sell-by date.

Time To Throw In The Towel

Among the early dates I had was one with a former boxer. We chatted online for several weeks before I decided that he might be worthy of further investigation. At the time, it was quite usual for me to host a business meeting at a hotel and it never occurred to me that suggesting one as a venue for a first date could be easily misconstrued in this context.

I selected a seat in a booth in the bar area of a smart hotel to await the arrival of someone I secretly hoped might turn out to be a brighter version of Rocky Balboa. When a face I recognised only partially started to approach me it certainly was enough to cause my heart to skip a couple of beats. The sudden erratic nature of my cardiac output, however, was not as a result of something pleasant. Further confirmation of this was provided by my bowels which had also become worryingly active for exactly the same reason. Bracing myself for impact, I quickly extended my hand hoping this would repel any attempt at a hug in favour of a more formal and less invasive greeting instead. Whatever pugilistic talents the scruffy-looking individual now taking up space in my booth might legitimately have laid claim to, were vastly exceeded by those associated with his extensive photoshopping ability. The only feature that had anything in common with the images that I had seen prior to our meeting was his nose.

The shape of this indicated that he probably was not too fleet of foot in the boxing ring either.

I responded to the boxer's offer to buy me a drink by requesting a glass of lemonade, as I definitely didn't want vodka to incline me towards a more favourable reassessment of my initial impressions. On too many occasions my favoured choice of tipple had caused me to behave in ways I later came to regret once sober again and I was determined to be more vigilant, especially in light of the company I now found myself in.

Once the boxer returned from the bar with our drinks there were a few moments of awkward silence, where even I was lost for words. He then decided to break the ice by asking me if I had any pets to which I truthfully answered that I had not. Reaching inside his jacket pocket he took out his phone and started to stab at it with his fingers. This unwelcome development revealed not only that his fingernails were thick with grime but it introduced the distinct aroma of shit into the proceedings too. He followed up his first question with another by asking me if I would like to see a picture of his Fanny and Meatball and then thrust his phone into my face without bothering to wait for my response. The subsequent discovery that Fanny and Meatball were the names of his two pet ferrets was disturbing enough, but something of a relief under the circumstances.

My subsequent expression of incredulity seemed to have been interpreted by the boxer as one of interest. Operating under this misapprehension, he proceeded to tell me not only all about the antics of his duo of ferrets but that he also had an allotment where he produced above-average girth prize-winning marrows. I glanced at both my crystal-encrusted heels and long fingernails which were highly polished in the colour of antique silver and could only imagine why he thought I would be interested in either. I concluded that repeated blows to the head had adversely affected his judgment of people. Fearing that he might never notice my levels of disinterest which were now suggestive of someone in the advanced stages of rigor mortis, and convinced that the CO_2 in my glass of lemonade was about to induce a bout of episodic wind, I stood up to leave. He reached out, grasping my hand and gesturing skywards before asking me if I knew what was directly above us. I followed his gaze towards the ceiling and suggested that as it was pissing down outside and neither of us was wet, a roof was a bloody good bet. Completely oblivious to my sarcasm he cut straight to the chase and asked me if I would like to join him for a lie-down in one of the bedrooms upstairs. By now, to use a popular boxing analogy, I was floating like a butterfly and ready to sting like a Bee. I replied by saying that if chasing his Fanny and Meatball around the allotment all day had left him in need of a lie-down my Beaver and I were not in a similar need of repose so would not be joining him for one. Claiming a technical knockout, I threw in the towel on this encounter and resolved to rethink the wisdom of arranging a first date in a hotel going forward.

What follows next shows just how long that resolution lasted.

A Man In Uniform

Whilst some women are attracted to men in uniform, personally speaking, I have never had any particular inclination towards one. So, I was surprised to be drawn towards a profile picture in part, because of a smart military uniform. The guy wearing it was called Tony and had an impressive row of medals pinned to his expansive chest although quite frankly these could have been chocolate coins dangling from pieces of string for all I know about militaria. Tony described himself as looking for a genuine relationship now that his children were grown up and fully independent. He had been married only once and was divorced from the mother of his children, was well-travelled and had a keen interest in both his level of physical fitness and appearance. His response to my standard message arrived soon after I sent it and our initial communications seemed to confirm that Tony was at least literate.

I couldn't find the existence of any red flags that suggested that it would be unwise to swap phone numbers with him and our subsequent conversations did not reveal the presence of any that I might have missed. After several weeks of chatting, we agreed to meet up to see where things might go from there.

Despite the assumptions of the boxer, I went ahead and arranged to meet Tony at another hotel bar, this time in the seaside town of Blackpool on the Fylde coast. In my defence, I was scheduled to be in this area for several days to attend a series of previously arranged business meetings, so I managed to justify this decision to myself on the grounds of convenience. I was also hoping that the many distractions available to us in the home of the *Kiss Me Quick* hat and the world-famous *Golden Mile* would keep us busy for an afternoon, after which Tony would take the train home again as planned.

I checked myself into the hotel after a morning meeting, which left me with plenty of time to orientate myself. I was quite relaxed at the prospect of meeting Tony and maybe even a tad excited by the handsome features of the chap in his photographs, providing of course, that he didn't possess the same photoshopping expertise as his pugilistic predecessor.

With so much time to spare before our date, I decided there were worse ways to kill it than indulging in a small aperitif while I waited. In those days my overnight bag was equipped with a litre bottle of vodka as standard, so I poured myself what I considered was a fairly modest measure. Such was the level of my self-delusion back then, it was probably more the equivalent of a large double. I settled into a comfortable seat by the window in my lovely all-expenses paid suite to watch the waves rolling onto the beach opposite. The Irish Sea has little in common with the colour and clarity of the ocean that hugs the shoreline of the Gulf of Mexico, but as I watched the gentle undulations of the waves I was momentarily transported back to another time and place.

I remembered when Kenny and I would sit beside each other to watch yet another stunning sunset on our beloved island of Captiva, content in our mutual and silent appreciation of the moments when no words were necessary. Engulfed by the memories that rolled in with the tide of when we had been blissfully ignorant of the horrors that lay in wait, it was inevitable that the eyeliner I applied with such meticulous precision only moments earlier would be quickly destroyed by tears. I reached for my makeup mirror so that I could repair the damage, annoyed that the defences I had worked so hard on fortifying since losing Kenny had been breached with such ease. I gasped, shocked by the image that stared back at me from the very depths of the mirror of a woman sitting alone in her anonymous hotel room drinking from a lipstick-stained glass and waiting to meet a complete stranger. Deeply repelled by the sight of this broken and tired old lady whose image I refused to equate with myself, despite the evidence of my own eyes, I reached for my overnight bag. As I tried to force all of my self-loathing into it in order to leave, I was further frustrated by the realisation that I was already unfit to drive. Grabbing the bottle of vodka, I continued to plan my escape, this time by making use of a different, but familiar, mode of transport.

The alcohol soon began to work its cruel magic and gradually the feelings of grief and anger began to dissipate in favour of something distinctly lighter and more welcome. I managed to fix my eyeliner, albeit, with none of the precision of earlier, and even congratulated myself for having the strength of spirit to stage a comeback. The credit for this, of course, was owed to the spirit in the 37.5% proof alcohol rather than any of my own. I performed a final check on my make-up and pouting like a prize-winning trout, I applied another slick of bright lipstick, drained my glass and prepared myself for my very first audition at the seaside.

I didn't notice Tony enter the bar because I was engrossed in both another large vodka and the banality of social media which I was scrolling through on my phone. Being caught completely off guard by the feel of his hand touching my shoulder I leapt up to hug him as though we had just been reunited at an airport. Quickly regaining my composure, I apologised for my over-exuberance which, if it had taken him by surprise, he was able to conceal. He motioned towards my glass offering to refill it which given that I am by nature an optimist was surprisingly half empty yet again. Any remaining vestiges of my self-control had long since vacated the building, with my biggest fear now being that my glass would be replenished with a single measure of vodka and not the double, I was too embarrassed to request. Instead, I insisted that Tony take a seat while I went to the bar to buy the drinks. My first impressions of him were favourable. He was every bit as handsome as his profile pictures had promised and I resolved to try harder to regain at least some of my errant self-control. Towards this end, I tried hard to disguise my level of intoxication beneath a non-stop stream of witty repartee. I convinced myself that the grin on Tony's face was evidence of the fact that this tactic was working well. In truth, it was far more likely that the ex-soldier thought the drunk widow opposite might not be the relationship prospect he was looking for, but might still have the potential for a connection on a far more basic level.

Keen to avoid being invited for another lie-down, albeit this would have been a lot more tempting given how attractive Tony was, I suggested that we took a stroll along the seafront. I assumed that his cool response to the idea was because he was considerably behind me in the alcohol stakes and might have preferred to sink a few more pints as opposed to the taking in of some bracing sea air instead. He half-heartedly agreed to my suggestion and, as I followed him outside, I noticed for the first time that he walked with a very awkward gait. This appeared to be because he leaned sharply over to one side as in the well-known tower of a similar inclination. Not entirely sure that this wasn't some kind of an optical illusion brought on by all the vodka, I could only hope that he might straighten up again once I started to sober up.

However, as we started to walk along the promenade it became increasingly clear that he found it a struggle to walk normally. His steps were tentative and faltering, although my curiosity as to why, was overridden by the need for me to concentrate on walking in a straight line myself. Occasionally I would try to level my stride with the inclusion of a few impromptu skips which unfortunately rather than disguising my unsteadiness were unhelpfully reminiscent of Charlie Chaplin's famous drunken walk. Despite this and Tony perambulating with all the speed of a snail, we managed to cover a surprising amount of distance before it began to rain quite heavily. Both grateful for the excuse to seek shelter from the rain, we decided to have lunch in a bar on the pier.

I was confused as to why Tony had gone to such lengths to present himself as a fitness fanatic when it was clear that even my limited athletic ability was superior to his. I decided that I would ask him outright what his difficulties were. He explained, looking more than a little sheepish, that some years previously he had undergone back surgery which had left him with a severe curvature of the spine. He apologised profusely for not mentioning any of this before, but he thought had he done so it might have put me off meeting him. No shit Sherlock! The experience of caring for my mother throughout my childhood and of course that of losing my husband ordinarily means that I am sympathetic to those struggling with health issues. The fact that Tony hadn't been honest with me concerning his, however, had presented me with something of a fait accompli and was not something I appreciated.

Deciding that a walk back to the hotel was beyond our capabilities for entirely different reasons, we elected to hop on a tram instead. Tony struggled to climb aboard and navigate his way towards a seat, so thankfully wasn't aware of what happened as I followed him. I misjudged my grip on the boarding stanchion which forced me to swivel around it several times like an elderly pole dancer, exposing my underwear to other passengers in the process. Once we were both seated and fighting to bring our respiratory rates back into a normal range, we resorted to sign language when pointing out the famous Blackpool landmarks en route.

The scenery started to look more familiar and I realised that we were nearly back at the hotel. I did consider making a quick disembarkation from the tram and bidding farewell to Tony then and there, but given the spectacular nature of my entrance, I could not guarantee that my exit would be any less entertaining. In any event the prospect of returning to my hotel alone without the distraction of something to quieten the demands of my inner grief which kept on insisting that I face it, was also just too big a risk. When it came to the choice of spending the evening in the company of a disabled and dishonest stranger or the broken old woman lying in wait for me in my room was yet another fait accompli which this time was accepted with gratitude.

I have little memory of what happened after I made the decision to invite Tony back to the hotel for more drinks. All I do know is that when I awoke the following morning my head was pounding and my mouth felt like a sandpit. The light flooding in from the window hurt my eyes as I tried to figure out where I was before the hazy recollections of the previous evening began to filter through. Cringing with embarrassment I recalled dancing in the hotel bar with the type of wild abandon you might employ when you think no one is watching except, of course, they were, with several people telling me to sit down and behave. I tried to sit up but the new perspective on my spinning surroundings revealed further new horrors to behold in the process. A jacket several sizes too big for it to have been one of mine was slung over the back of a chair and the sound of running water coming from the bathroom provided more evidence of the fact that I was not alone. I don't think I have ever felt as far removed from the person I had been in my entire life with Kenny than I did at that moment. I peered under the duvet and discovered that I was naked except for my industrial-strength Spanx, which were thankfully still in situ. This, I dared to hope, might be an indication that whoever it was enjoying a nice warm shower in my suite this morning had found them to be as impenetrable as I found them supportive.

Then I caught sight of several files on a nearby table and remembered that the primary purpose of my trip had been for business. The bathroom door opened and, wrapped in nothing but a towel, Tony bade me a cheery good morning. I noted that he was still leaning to one side as he started to make his way back towards the bed. Determined that whatever had not happened last night was certainly not going to be happening this morning, I tried to preserve what little remained of my modesty by wrapping the duvet tightly around me and slid off the bed with all the grace of a walrus. Once I reached the relative sanctity of the bathroom I began the all-too-regular routine that would help me not only clean up but sober up too.

When I returned to the bedroom Tony was fully dressed, probably having realised that without the encouraging effects of alcohol in large amounts I was unlikely to be as accommodating as I had been the night before. With precious little time left for pleasantries, I ushered him towards the door, apologised for my behaviour and explained that whether he believed it or not it was totally out of character. As I closed the door firmly behind him, I felt nothing other than relief that I had not come to any serious harm as a result of my liaison with him.

Death On The Farm

I met Danny, who was a farmer, on the site I joined that catered specifically for widows and widowers. His late wife had tragically died after a fall at their farmhouse after a very happy marriage of thirty years duration and, understandably, he was devastated by her death. Having the loss of a spouse in common did facilitate a certain ease of discussion when it came to talking about the difficulties of adjusting to life after losing one. Often, it's hard for those fortunate not to have gone through this experience themselves, to fully appreciate the complexities involved.

Danny said that, since the death of his wife, he had been on quite a few dates but, despite meeting some lovely women, had not been able to find that spark that has no tangible description but which we all recognise once we find it. During our conversations, it was apparent that he had a wicked sense of humour, although I did suspect that on occasion his skilled and witty banter owed more than a little to a drop of the hard stuff. Given that much of my own relied on a similar crutch, I was certainly in no position to judge him for that.

After the usual round of messages and phone calls, Danny and I agreed that we would meet up for a lunch date. We chose a lovely country pub not far from his farm, because it was en route to a friend of mine, whom I intended to visit later on that day.

As usual, I arrived at my destination, a beautifully quaint country village, far earlier than was necessary, so I decided to have a snoop around the local village store/café in the meantime. I entered the shop and smiled to myself when, as is often the case in tight-knit communities, conversations are momentarily paused to observe the arrival of an unfamiliar face in their midst. There was every manner of merchandise inside this hub of the local community, including freshly baked bread, jars of speciality homemade jams and beautifully packaged boxes of shortbread, one of which I decided to buy as a gift for my friend. As I made my way to the till to pay for it, I noticed something that had me reaching for one of the two pairs of glasses that are always perched on the top of my head and helped bring a local newspaper headline into much sharper focus.

Local man quizzed by police after wife's fatal fall at farmhouse.

Both my eyes and mouth widened simultaneously as I recognised the face in the picture as none other than the same Danny that I was here to have lunch with. I grabbed the newspaper and my throat went dry as I read the details of how his wife had died as the result of a fall at their home, just as he had said. What he had failed to mention, though, was that she had broken her neck after falling down a staircase during a drunken argument and it was suspected that he had pushed her. I remembered now my own suspicions concerning Danny's liking for a drink and my heart pounded as I read the rest of the newspaper report. What was also very apparent on reading it was that all of this had happened far more recently than Danny had led me to believe. So recently, in fact, that should she have been exhumed the poor woman might still have registered a temperature! I couldn't believe that I had discussed the struggles of being a widow/widower with a man who had not only been one for five bloody minutes, but who might have been responsible for this unfortunate change in his marital circumstances as a result of his own actions. I grabbed a copy of the newspaper, and my shortbread, adding a large bottle of vodka to my list of purchases, before making my way quickly back to the car and tearing off in the direction of my friend's house, burning rubber like one of the Dukes of Hazzard.

I blocked any further contact from Danny and I never heard of him again. To this day I have no idea if he was just the victim of unfortunate circumstances and some salacious village gossip or, indeed, something altogether more sinister. Either way, Danny was, at the very least, guilty of indecent haste when it came to the speed at which he had started his search for a replacement for his poor deceased wife.

Is internet dating worth the effort?

I have not recorded the details of all of the first dates I went on or those that were aborted during take-off. This is not just because it would necessitate a book the size of an Encyclopaedia Britannica to do so, but because they are far too tedious to consider inflicting the monotonous details on anyone else.

A common thread running through the vast majority of those first dates, however, was the dishonesty of the men involved, which ranged from little white lies to those that were far darker in colour. This is confirmed in the following few examples.

One guy who claimed to be a professional paramedic turned out to be a volunteer for the St Johns ambulance brigade in his spare time instead, as revealed by a quick search of his social media. Another appeared to suffer from amnesia when it came to remembering the number of children he had. He was happy to lay claim to two of them from his previous relationship, but again the long arm of the internet revealed the existence of another four, all of whom he had fathered with different mothers. Then there was Popeye, so named because he had been in the Royal Navy. During our date at a busy music venue, he insisted on following me to the toilet, for my own safety. On the way back from one of these interludes someone accidentally spilt his drink over my white jumpsuit, which caused Popeye to react as though he had just discovered that Bluto had buggered Olive Oyl. Suffice it to say, this was another first date that was not followed by a second. My point here is that despite scrutinising the minutiae of any *profile* that you come across on a dating site, there will always come that point where you simply have to *suck it and see,* which I freely admit is not the most carefully chosen metaphor in these circumstances.

We have all read about the success stories concerning couples who are lucky enough to meet quickly and then go on to form loving relationships. It is worth remembering, though, that a lot of these so-called success stories are generated by the sites themselves. Ultimately, for most of us trying to find someone compatible on a dating site, it will require a little more than the intervention of lady luck. I understand why people become disheartened with this method of trying to find companionship, friendship or even love. Dating sites are a difficult place to navigate, frequented as they are, by the romance fraudsters already highlighted. Even men who do not fall into this specific category are often not who we had hoped they might be. On top of this, as in my case, our late spouses may have already set an incredibly high bar, making the effort involved in meeting someone else in this way seem pointless.

I consider myself to be one of life's optimists, but just like anyone else I have experienced some very dark times in my life. Throughout, I have always prided myself on my ability to bounce back and this positive attitude was to serve me well when it came to internet dating, which requires both stamina and persistence.

Internet dating gave me not only a purpose that led to the publishing of this book, but was also one of the vehicles I used to avoid the process of grieving for my late husband. Any of the pain I inflicted on myself, as a consequence of my exploits with any of the men I met online, paled into insignificance by comparison. I also subscribe to the school of thought which believes *that which doesn't kill you makes you stronger*. Had I given up on internet dating, I might not have found the happiness that was waiting in the wings for me as a result of both persistence and good fortune.

Chapter 6

Alan

A Laugh A Minute And Much More

Of the five of my aforementioned categories, the one entitled *The If's, But's and Maybe's* contained the profiles of the men who I hoped had the most relationship potential. Alan's was one such profile.

His wicked sense of humour was evident in his very first message and my response to it led to an exchange of missives that invariably reduced me to tears of laughter as I read them and sometimes even before I had.

The decision to exchange our contact details was a relatively easy one, although it probably shouldn't have been, given that it was made purely on the basis of Alan's ability to make me laugh like a drain. For all I knew outside of this, he could have been a serial killer whose targeted victims had literally curled up and died with laughter.

If I did have any concerns at all, it was only that Alan might not be as verbally engaging over the phone as he had been throughout our exchange of written messages. These concerns, however, were quickly dispelled during our first conversation in which he revealed himself to be every bit as witty as I'd hoped. He possessed a warmth and cheeky charm that I found quite endearing, and even reminded me of Kenny, although I always tried to avoid comparisons with the incomparable. The pattern of our conversations was always the same, in that they were heavily punctuated by regular bouts of hysterical laughter. All too often this would cause us to lose all track of time, so it was not unusual for us to still be chatting well into the early hours. If ever proof was needed concerning the physiological benefits of laughter, then Alan and I were the embodiment of that proof. After I started talking to him, I couldn't deny the presence of an extra spring in my step that hadn't been there since I lost Kenny. Alan would only admit to feeling about six months younger than his birth certificate insisted he was as a result of his talking to me, although he did say that he hadn't even been expecting even this modest change.

Because of the endless stream of banter going back and forth between us, it took some time for us to learn anything tangible about each other. It transpired that Alan had been married and divorced twice, with both of his ex-wives not only taking a sizeable chunk of the businesses he had built up from scratch, but also a big bite out of his ability to trust women in the same way again.

There was an issue with distance too, in that there was roughly a two-hundred-mile commute between our two locations. Alan's businesses required him to work unsociable hours, which, when combined with my commitments at the time, meant that planning a date was never going to be an easy task. Until a suitable opportunity presented itself, we were content in the meantime with the phone calls that quickly became the highlight of both our days, to the extent that we would both panic if something were to prevent us from talking to each other.

With the benefit of hindsight, delaying our first date for as long as we did, was probably what dealt our relationship a fatal blow from which there was never any real chance of recovery. During this interim period, I was still speaking to several guys online, in the process of researching this book and never expected that Alan wouldn't carry on chatting with other ladies under these circumstances.

The Straw That Broke The Camel's Back

Harry was a solicitor who had been asking to meet up with me for some time until, more out of curiosity than anything else, I finally agreed that I would do so. I told Alan of my decision, and he insisted that I should go and have a good time. He added that coincidentally he was taking some of his employees on a team bonding exercise to the local zoo on the same afternoon that I arranged to meet Harry, but that we should catch up as usual later that evening. Because my young grandson had fallen in love with Mumble, the adorable penguin of Happy Feet fame, I asked Alan to send me some pictures of penguins if he got the chance and told him to enjoy himself too.

I made my way to the large outdoor retail outlet that Harry and I had designated as a mutually convenient place to meet. It was a beautiful sunny day, which helped to bolster my mood, which, frankly, until I reached my destination and saw the fabulous array of shops, had been one of indifference. A spot of retail therapy is never far from the top of my list of ways to while away a couple of hours, so even if the date with Harry turned out to be a busted flush, it still had the potential to be salvageable. On arrival I sat myself down on a bench outside the store where we arranged to meet, to enjoy the sunshine and indulge in one of my favourite pastimes of people-watching.

Earning points for punctuality, I spotted a man making his way towards me, whose appearance was entirely consistent with the images I had seen on his profile, which was definitely a positive start. I got up from the bench and Harry leaned in to ignore my extended hand in favour of a hug, accompanied by a wet slobbery kiss, which he planted firmly on the side of my cheek. It was inevitable that, after being forced into such close proximity with him, I would discover Harry suffered from the worst case of halitosis I have ever had the misfortune to come into contact with. Taken aback by the pungent smell of what could only be described as similar to the collective breath of a thousand camels, I was also momentarily blinded by tears caused by this almost visible odour. I dabbed at my eyes and, before I had the chance to refocus them properly, Harry took me by the hand and announced that it was time for us to hit the shops. Without further warning, he then proceeded to drag me along beside him in a manner that left me not entirely sure that I wasn't about to become the victim of a kidnap attempt that was being executed in plain sight.

Undeterred, the strident solicitor insisted that we visit several stores of his choosing, without stopping to enquire if I might have any preferences of my own. After spending some time lurching from store to store, hardly able to hear what he was saying over the sound of my screeching heels, I suggested we might take a break and enjoy a small glass of something refreshing, hoping that this would give me time to re-group and reassess. During this interval, it became clear that Harry's favourite topic of conversation was himself. He appeared to have no interest in me other than as someone who was prepared to sit and listen to him drone on about his favourite subject.

During this lengthy monologue, I learned that he had never married, despite several long-term relationships. He now lived alone with his cat Harriet, whose name I suspect owed much to the high level of self-esteem in which he held himself. He also claimed to be a workaholic who was passionate about his work. This resulted in a brief spark of interest, as I imagined his work to be something important such as reforming the Human Rights Act. In truth, I have no idea how anyone could say that they were passionate about conveyancing which turned out to be the branch of legal work that he was involved with. When he wasn't busy dealing with the banal complexities of the land registry, he spent his spare time quizzing with a local pub team as their captain.

Inexplicably, he would periodically interrupt this mind-numbing presentation of his potted life history by leaning over to give me a peck on the cheek, as though we were a well-established couple and not the total strangers that we actually were. Of course, each time that this happened the undeniable stench of eau-de-camel was overwhelmingly disgusting, so I decided that it was high time to cut my losses and get the heck out of Dodge. I finished my drink as Harry continued to drone on in blissful ignorance of the fact that his audience was about to depart the auditorium and patiently waited for a suitable pause to announce my impending departure. When it did, I thanked him for inviting me to meet him, but I didn't think that we were likely to share much in common, so it probably wasn't worth wasting any more of each other's time. I also wished him well and hoped that he had a safe journey back to Harriet, whilst secretly hoping the poor little moggie had no sense of smell.

Harry's reaction was to shrug his shoulders in disbelief, looking genuinely shocked by my decision to cut our date short, before saying that it was a shame that I was leaving because he thought we had been getting along swimmingly. Now it was my turn to be bemused, not least because I had not been invited to contribute any information about myself and had hardly even spoken at all up until this point. In his determination to prove me wrong about having nothing in common, he cited what he saw as our mutual enjoyment of the same types of stores, before adding that he also thought I was a very good listener. This, he added, was a rare quality in a woman these days, as he often found them to be self-absorbed and guilty of constant interruptions when he was talking. Apparently, he found my polite acquiescence refreshing and something he was looking for in a partner. Anyone who knows me will attest to the fact that I don't do *polite acquiescence* unless I have suffered some kind of serious medical event that has robbed me of my ability to speak. I considered just walking away at this point, feeling that any response on my part was probably futile. However, I wanted to demonstrate that his appraisal of my personality was grossly inaccurate and that my inability to *politely acquiesce* often caused the fool in me to go where angels feared to tread.

I explained that if he had taken the trouble to even try to get to know me, he might have discovered that I was actually a woman who held strong opinions on a range of subjects and was not at all afraid of expressing them when prompted, or indeed even when I wasn't. My opinion concerning his 1950s attitude towards women, for instance, was unlikely to be what he wanted to hear and probably the stuff of his worst nightmares. As for his assumption that I had derived any pleasure whatsoever from our visit to the Edinburgh woollen mill, when I would have preferred to purchase a stick of candy floss over a tartan blanket any day, all suggested that we had jack shit in common. As far as I was concerned all of this was irrefutable evidence, which, as a lawyer, even he might have had a hard time dismissing in court.

It was hardly a shock that Harry did not possess the social skills necessary to deal graciously with anyone who was not in agreement with his views, especially when that dissension came from a mere woman. Feeling that there was little to be gained by prolonging the discussion any further I got up to leave, but Harry was determined to have the last word. His parting shot was to loudly announce that I was surprisingly confident for a fat girl, but at least now he wouldn't have the embarrassment of having to introduce an obese person to his pub quiz team. His outburst, as it was clearly designed to do, aroused the attention of a small but curious audience, who I was determined would not leave this particular drama disappointed by a lacklustre ending.

So, I reached inside my handbag and started to spray my breath freshener into the air as though I was in charge of a fire extinguisher on the film set of The Towering Inferno, before handing him the empty spray and urging him to buy some to help neutralise the effects of his camel breath. Ensuring that I could be heard by everyone, even those in cheap seats, I urged him to keep using it until he could figure out what it was that had died in his stomach. I then took my leave of both halitosis Harry and an amused but satisfied audience in my wake.

The Mystery Of The Missing Penguins

If I should have been upset by Harry's behaviour towards me then I wasn't. Okay maybe the fat girl thing stung a bit, especially when I had lost a considerable amount of weight by this time. All I wanted to do was to get home as soon as possible so that I could tell Alan what had happened, knowing how hilarious he would have found it. Several hours later, though, I still hadn't heard from him, which was quite unusual, and I was disappointed not to have received even one penguin picture.

It did occur to me that the absence of a penguin picture might be because Alan had not been to visit the zoo after all, as he had claimed. Maybe, he had been on a date too and, given how I had spent my day, the feeling in the pit of my stomach was a little hard to fathom. I also struggled to understand, if this was the case, why Alan hadn't just been truthful with me, as we both usually were.

Deep down, though, I also understood that whatever it was that existed between us was at times exhausting to preserve. It also restricted us from pursuing something more tangible and normal.

Sometime later Alan's number finally flashed up on my caller ID and he sounded as bright and breezy as ever and desperate to know all the gory details of my date with the solicitor. I told him I would be happy to tell him all about it, but that he should tell me all about his date first. I could hear him take a deep breath, after a momentary pause, he sheepishly admitted to having spent the afternoon in the company of a charming and attractive lady who lived quite close by. I knew then that the discomfort in my lower midriff was caused by a good old-fashioned case of the green-eyed monster. Alan apologised unreservedly for not being truthful with me and then asked if I would mind him asking me a question. Given that he didn't usually seek such permission before asking me anything, I braced myself for what might be about to come. In the end, he simply asked me if I believed that it was possible to fall in love with someone that you had never actually met. Before this, my answer to this question would have been an unequivocal no, but now I answered honestly that I thought yes, it very well might be.

He responded by saying that we needed to know once and for all what it was that we did or didn't have going on between us. I knew that he was right, as we concluded what proved to be our shortest-ever phone conversation.

Post Penguin Gate

Thanks to a timely lesson taught by the absence of a penguin and still struggling to identify just what it was that we felt for each other, Alan and I moved heaven and earth in our efforts to re-arrange our busy schedules so that we could meet at last. During this process, we had cause to cancel our arrangements many times over, which took us right back to square one. I came to realise that these procrastinations had much more to do with the emotional complexities involved rather than any of those of a logistical nature. Finding ourselves constantly bounced back to square one would not have been tolerated by either one of us had this happened in our professional lives, but in this context, square one was a known and comfortable quantity. Square one was a place of safety where, unburdened by the humdrum requirements of everyday life, we existed in our own bubble, free to choose the best bits of each other to like and love without any of those other influences.

The price of existing within the safety of this sphere, however, had come at the cost of a commitment to meet in person. To do so now was to take the risk of the bubble bursting, and us both losing something we regarded to be invaluable as a consequence.

The Bubble Meets The Pin

When I did finally meet Alan, it was like greeting an old friend that you haven't seen in a long while, which in many ways is exactly what he was, except for the fact that I hadn't seen him ever. We both giggled like two teenagers at first sight of each other and it was a struggle to manage the sensory overload that came with being able to see, touch and even smell each other for the first time. There were no thunderbolts of lightning or fireworks, just a deep sense of satisfaction and joy that, even as a writer, I cannot properly find the words to articulate. Despite this, I sensed already that our paths were probably destined to continue on the same parallel as they had been before we had taken a pin to our bubble.

What if?

The pragmatic difficulties posed by the distance between our respective locations continued to play havoc with the logistics of being able to meet up on a regular basis. When we did manage to overcome these, the time we spent together was always more than worth the effort and we still had our nightly phone calls to sustain us in between times. The problem of trying to nurture a fledgling relationship that held so much in the way of potential, but still could not properly take flight, forced us both to face the answers to some very difficult questions. We explored every possible permutation that would allow us to be together more often, most of which required a huge commitment on either part as there were no half-measures available to us in any of the *what-if* scenarios we explored.

Because of Alan's business interests, re-location was not a feasible option for him, and, not unreasonably, he was also wary of upping sticks and starting all over again based on what happened with both of his ex-wives. I was restricted by my own commitments too at the time, which were not portable either, although I am not sure that, even if they had been, I would have chosen this option.

I knew that I felt love for Alan but struggled to fully define what this meant and how and if I should make changes to my life to even try to understand it. It is often said of love that if it is meant to be, then it will be, regardless of any attempt at tinkering around the edges of what fate has already decreed will happen. We had both been advised by family and friends, who all subscribed to the view that all of the difficulties standing in our way could be overcome if we just loved one another enough. Maybe this somewhat romanticised view is true for some people, but I think for us the key lay in the word enough. At our ages, life's hurdles tend to look a little bit higher than they might have in our younger days and certainly require more effort to clear. Just as we feared it might, once our bubble had burst and forced us back into the real world, we had our final confirmation that what we had between us was never designed to exist there.

Alan was a massive positive in my life and helped me through a period of transition which undoubtedly played a huge part in helping me to become who I am now. This, I believe, was the purpose of our connection and not that of a serious relationship, which fate forced us into recognising in the fullness of time.

The following is a piece I wrote for the original GOWNS website concerning one of our joint escapades.

The Tale Of Two Tattoos

I don't consider myself to be much of a conformist. What I mean by this is that ideologically I don't tend to respond particularly well to figures of autocracy. Political correctness, red tape and bureaucracy will often evoke and provoke a passionate response from yours truly.

However, despite this propensity, I remain essentially a middle-aged woman who buys her knickers from unethical sources because they are cheap, which makes me a raging hypocrite on this socio-economic issue and many others.

When I was younger having a tattoo, or an inking as it is now referred to, was the ultimate act of rebellion for a teenager who wanted to properly piss off a parent. I didn't choose this particular method of insinuating that I wished I had been adopted for several reasons, but primarily because someone else had thought of it first.

My kids, however, couldn't wait to avail themselves of Tramp Stamps as soon as they could walk to the tattoo parlour unaided and forge my signature on the consent forms. I will admit that the sight of the badly drawn images forever engraved on their tender young skin in indelible ink had the desired effect of pissing me off big time. I was suitably rebuked by both of them as they insisted they were simply expressing themselves through body art and I should embrace this instead of making my disapproval clear at every opportunity.

Fast forward a couple of decades and over time I did indeed begin to form an appreciation of the form of body art formerly known as getting a tatt.

After Kenny died, I decided to write a book about my experiences as a widow and, as a part of this, I intended to include those garnered from my time spent on a dating site. During this process, I met one great guy who like me, had never had, or wanted a tattoo. One night after quaffing our way through a bucket of Chablis and discussing how current attitudes to tattoos had changed making them more acceptable, we decided that this was the time to stage a middle-aged rebellion and go and get ourselves inked at the first available opportunity.

I was working on the concept of GOWNS, a website for grieving overwhelmed widows negotiating stuff at the time and knew that I would like to include this somewhere in my tattoo, along with a stiletto shoe as a reminder to keep both my standards and my heels high. Well, one out of two wasn't bad. I intended that the letter K would scroll around the heel of the shoe, symbolic of the fact that he had always been the anchor at my heel.

My partner in crime already had a good idea of what he wanted to see on his arm for the rest of his life, and all I will say about his choice, in light of the dire results of this football team, is that he should have chosen Accrington Stanley.

We arrived at the tattoo parlour. I don't know why they call a shop frequented by huge burly guys featuring more pictorial content on their bodies than the Tate Gallery a parlour, but the incongruence between purpose and name was enough to reduce my accomplice and me into fits of giggles.

Both thrilled with the results of enduring some mild discomfort, we were positive that the reaction to our new tattoos had much to offer yet in terms of entertainment value. We parried enquiries concerning how we had spent our day with deliberately vague answers to my curious offspring. Then we rolled up our sleeves and waited for the response that was all but inevitable once our new tattoos were made available for comment.

They were noticed by the eldest sibling first, who then proceeded at warp speed to inform the younger one of her discovery. This was swiftly followed by howls of protestation from both of them shortly after I confirmed that they were indeed looking at two examples of body art, through which my co-conspirator and I wished to express ourselves. As a reaction to the thinly veiled accusations of coercion that were levelled in his direction, my poor companion's complexion rapidly paled, though he quickly received the appropriate apologies from both of my offspring, as they knew better than most that I do not do undue influence.

Whilst I have always been opinionated and had the heart of a rebel my opportunities to act on these tendencies had been restricted by my mother's ill health throughout my childhood and teenage years. It brought it home to me just what I had missed, but what I was witnessing now went a long way to making up for that.

Apparently, our tattoos were an embarrassment, and it was obvious that we hadn't even thought about how they might look on our already wrinkled skin as we continued to age. Oh, the irony of youth.

In their defence, I suspect the unease with which they reacted to my having a boyfriend and a tattoo owed more to their unease with who I was becoming since Kenny's death rather than to any real objection to the tattoo itself. I was not the person who lived in the kitchen anymore, baking endless supplies of cookies and leaving it only to clean up or otherwise facilitate the smooth running of a family. My rebellion was late in coming to the party and must have been quite alarming to witness, but it was as necessary to my survival as the air I breathed.

As I write this, I have no idea what the future may hold as I continue to face life with a smile on my face and now a tattoo on my wrist. I do know, however, that my accomplice in this escapade is a big part of the reason that I am strong today and for that, I thank him from the bottom of my heart.

Chapter 7

Phil

You Got A Friend In Me

Most of the men who made it into my If's But's And Maybe's category usually qualified to be included on one criterion alone. Having a well-developed sense of humour and the ability to not take yourself too seriously is more important to me than either looks or money, although of course, they are a welcome bonus. The connection that Alan and I made through our joint appreciation of humour was always going to be a very hard act to follow, but the majority of my dates were all with men who had a good sense of humour, even when this proved to be the only thing we had in common.

Phil definitely possessed the requisite sense of humour and was also a man who was adept at making the lady in his company feel as though they were the only other person in the room. He was a tall athletic type, although, for reasons neither of us could quite understand given that we each ticked a lot of boxes for each other, we were only mildly attracted to each other in the physical sense.

Situated geographically much nearer to where I was living than had been the case with Alan, Phil and I were able to meet up on a fairly regular basis. After a couple of months, we settled into what was a very pleasant friends-with-benefits type of arrangement. Not that I was aware that this is what it was at the time. Before Phil, I didn't even know that such a thing existed and, had I done so, I certainly would not have considered myself to be a candidate for one. I suppose that the truth of it is we both realised fairly early on that our relationship was never destined to be a deeply romantic one, but we really enjoyed each other's company and saw no reason not to carry on doing so. During my time with Phil, I always felt safe and well cared for in his company and any manipulative practices within the confines of our relationship were entirely equitable.

The Garden

I once wrote that Kenny was not an especially keen gardener, but that his efforts were sufficient to see to it that our garden always looked presentable and well-kept. It was only after he died that I had any real appreciation of the effort that went into maintaining this status quo. When I discovered that plain old grass can grow to heights well above that which I assumed was possible, my shock was entirely genuine. This necessitated some remedial action on my part involving the operation of a lawn mower for the first time. Unfortunately, my ineptitude with machines of any denomination resulted in injuries sufficiently egregious for me to decide that I no longer wanted or needed a garden.

Once in a while, I had cause to rethink my decision to abandon what was after all a sizeable chunk of outside space. These occasions were rare and usually short-lived, though, because of the garden's strong association with happier times, the reminders of which, were often too much for me to bear.

Deciding one afternoon that the promise of some glorious sunshine and an aperitif al fresco style was worth the risk of a memory ambush, I flattened an area of waist-high grass large enough to accommodate my lounger. The residual tall grass around it provided a perfect privacy screen shielding me from the prying eyes of my nosey neighbours. As I lay there sipping from my glass, with my face bathed in warm sunshine, I imagined for a moment that I was back on our beloved island of Captiva and I could almost hear the sound of the brown pelicans reeling overhead and see Kenny fishing with our two young grandsons on the T-dock. Tears found their way down my face and landed with a soggy splash into my ears. I tried to stifle a sob that caught the back of my throat and which I feared might alert the neighbours to my presence when my phone started to gently buzz in my pocket. Grateful for the timely distraction, I answered Phil who was clearly very excited about something and was insisting that he had just had the most amazing idea. I had to ask him several times to calm down to have any chance of understanding that he was proposing we should take a trip together. I looked up towards the clear blue sky, looking for a clue as to where this particular bolt had come from and my initial reaction was to dismiss his suggestion out of hand. I pointed out that we hadn't known each other that long and, although we got along just fine, a holiday where we would be in each, other's company 24/7 was a whole other ball game. This, of course, was the sensible side of me talking, which is all too often overruled by the far less sensible aspects of my personality, especially when encouraged to do so by alcohol. Phil continued to insist that an adventure spent with a mate was a great idea. He said he wasn't asking me to pick out curtains or anything, just to go away on holiday and have some fun. Struggling to find much of a counterargument past the word *adventure,* a noun always designed to appeal to someone like me and something Kenny told me that I should continue to seek out after he was gone, I eventually agreed to go.

I don't think the fact that I was on one of my rare excursions into the garden when I received Phil's invitation was a coincidence. The garden had been the custodian of so many precious and sometimes painful reminders of the past, but was now also the birthplace of new ones yet to be made. I didn't fully appreciate it at the time, but this was another important step in finding out who I was going to be without my husband of thirty-six years at my side.

The following is another article I wrote for the original GOWNS website in 2016 before Phil and I left for our trip to Las Vegas.

Holiday Shoes June 27th 2016

Ooookay people...the holiday season is upon us but for GOWNS going on holiday for the first time without our spouse or partner can be a very daunting prospect.

I was lucky in that I was able to negotiate my first holiday without Kenny with Jayne, my dear friend and collaborator in GOWNS. Yes, there were the inevitable tears during that most poignant of firsts but thanks to our mutual understanding of what had caused them, they dried without the need for apologies or explanations making things much easier for us than they might otherwise have been.

Somewhat unexpectedly I am now facing the negotiation of another holiday, this time in the company of a male friend. OK, he's a bit more than a friend and a bit less than a boyfriend but these are mere semantics. In just a few short weeks I will be taking to the skies once again, this time bound for the Nevada desert to visit Las Vegas. This might seem a strange choice of destination for someone who has always been disinclined towards any kind of slot machine thrill and thought that chips were something you ate on your way back from the pub, but was chosen for a couple of reasons. Kenny and I spent a lot of time in the USA and it still feels very much like a second home to me, and also because my travelling companion had never been to America but has always wanted to go. The glittering heat haze that hangs over the strip during the day and gives way to the spectacular display of neon lighting that straddles it by night was another thing we wanted to witness for ourselves. Vegas is also home to some of the best stages, eateries and casinos in the world and is unashamedly unapologetic about the hedonistic nature of its raison d'etre.

So, what are my main concerns when it comes to this trip? At the risk of exposing the true lack of depth in my shallow intellect, I have to tell you it is my shoes that are causing me to lose the most sleep at the moment. Maybe it should be the Brexit effect on my holiday dollars which should concern me more, but my footwear dilemma is the clear front-runner when it comes to things to worry about.

Dominated by heels high enough to trigger a nosebleed, my collection of shoes is significant in size. Having researched the vast scale of the territory I am about to traverse in Vegas, the casinos alone are the size of cities, I am concerned that my sparkly high heels may not be the most appropriate choice in these circumstances.

I am going to be staying at the Venetian on the strip which famously has a canal flowing through the middle of it and I am quite determined to partake in an experience with a gondolier. However, what shoes does one wear to ensure the graceful entry and exit of a gondola? It might seem obvious that sensible footwear is more suited to the task, but it also true that sensible equates to ugly when it comes to shoes.

On top of this conundrum, there is also the matter of my baggage allowance to consider. Crystal-encrusted shoes have nothing in common with a flip-flop in either an aesthetic or weight sense, with the former being fairly beefy in terms of grams. The prospect of having to leave them behind purely on the basis of their weight would be like trying to diet by way of amputation.

Having pondered this predicament for some time now I can happily conclude that the sparkly heels have it. I have set aside a sensible budget to cover the cost of buying any foot restorative products which may become necessary and fully intend that the best of my feet going forward in Vegas, will be clad in sparkles regardless of their suitability.

Now that little dilemma is solved, I have just ordered a beautiful pair of burnt orange heels which I think will look fabulous against the terracotta backdrop of the desert.

Play Therapy

As I re-read the above a couple of years after it was written, I have very mixed feelings about the version of me that penned it. I definitely detect some quite childish undertones in much of what I wrote back then but nowadays I have a better understanding of why that was.

My childhood was no place for a child in that my mother's illness forced both of my parents to rely on me as they would another adult. As a consequence, learning through play like any other child was not an option for me. Now, unburdened by responsibility for anyone other than herself the child who had been born an adult, finally had the opportunity to play and Phil proved to be a perfect playground partner.

The following article is another written before we left for our Vegas trip, which as I read it now makes me smile as I recognise the excitement of a middle-aged widowed woman, unfamiliar with herself as a person, free to be as childish as she liked at last.

Holiday Sums Not Adding Up July 06 2016

Oookay people...my trip to the grand old US of A is moving ever closer and simply put I am just not ready. My bedroom looks like the ladieswear department at Debenhams and I might need to bring the eviction of Kenny's clothes forward in order to create some space, something else I am not ready for either.

At least my current focus has shifted from my shoes to my bright and beautiful lime green suitcase. I chose it entirely on the basis of its appearance with scant regard for the fact that even when empty it is still heavier than a fully-laden sea-fairing trunk. To think that I once packed for a family of five and no one and nothing got left behind, I find my inability to do so now for myself alone, somewhat inexplicable.

On top of this, the Guilt Monkey has decided that now is a good time to remind me of some of the correct protocols for the execution of widow duties which are as follows:

1. Thou shalt not replace one's dead spouse with a casual substitute found on a dating site.

2. If you must insist on travelling to Las Vegas for the purposes of pleasure with said substitute, you should at least try not to enjoy doing so out of respect for all the widows who are grieving their husbands with some dignity.

3. Resolve to do better in future.

The Guilt Monkey, however, had seriously overestimated the effectiveness of his influence over my decisions by this stage in my grief journey. My responses to his attempt at persuading me to take a guilt trip instead of one leading to Las Vegas are as follows.

1. There could never be a substitute, casual, or otherwise, for my late husband and for now spending a holiday with someone I met on a dating site suits me just fine.

2. I see no merit in misery and neither did Kenny, accordingly I feel under no obligation to adhere to this unnecessary stereotype of how a widow should or shouldn't behave.

3. I had both the love and respect of my late husband as he had mine. Therefore, there will be no explanations concerning my behaviour either now or in the future.

*4. F*** off! I know there isn't a fourth point on your list but I felt the need for one in case anything in my other three responses was anything less than crystal clear.*

Maths has never been a strong point of mine but I can usually manage the basics for example 14 nights = 14 pairs of knickers + plus extras to cover emergencies. Simples, right? Except when you factor in the required functionality for these said items. How many big knickers designed for comfort does one include as opposed to those worn in more alluring circumstances? How many of each type are required?

Trying to find the correct permutation of shorts, dresses and swimwear has resulted in a selection of garments whose critical mass far exceeds the capacity of my suitcase. Therefore, the only solution I can find has come in the form of a perfectly pink companion for my lovely lime suitcase. It is highly likely now that I will arrive at the airport looking like the testcard that used to grace our television screens and still without an answer to the following mathematical equation.

1 Traveller + 2 suitcases + 1 hand luggage = How many arms?

Happy Landings

Our arrival in Las Vegas after a ten-hour flight was as amazing an experience as I expected it would be. The strip straddles up to eleven lanes in parts and the traffic moved from lane to lane without impunity. The discovery of each famous landmark we had only ever seen before in photographs prompted reactions from Phil and me that would have helped the cab driver confirm our status as first-time visitors and to adjust his cab fare accordingly.

When we arrived at the Venetian hotel it looked every bit as stunning as I hoped it would, though the level of this splendid opulence was in stark contrast to the sight of those begging out on the sidewalk nearby.

The following is another article I wrote after Phil and I had been in Vegas for a couple of days.

Fire, Ice And A Little White Lie

As I expected it might be on arrival, Vegas is revealing itself to be a place of huge contrasts, all of which seem to coexist in close proximity along the length of the famous strip. The high-rollers with their platinum credit cards sometimes lose amounts of money in the casinos that those begging outside on the sidewalks could only hope to earn in a year.

The searing heat here today has reached a staggering 117 degrees, which has caused the State Governors to announce an excessive heat warning. This might sound like a statement of the bleeding obvious, but when you spend a lot of your time in air-conditioned buildings it is very easy to under-estimate the ferocity of the heat outside.

Phil and I decided it was sensible to heed the warnings and avoid the heat by going to the other extreme and visiting a bar called Minus 5, which, as its name suggests, maintains a temperature of a decidedly chilly minus-five degrees. The bar and everything inside it is constructed completely from ice.

Once inside our wintry domain, we were persuaded to part with $150 in exchange for a VIP package which included the use of two fur coats for the duration of our visit and a Cossack hat each to keep. The hats were gifted on the condition that we did not wear them outside which might have been the most redundant request you are likely to hear when the temperatures are well in excess of one hundred degrees. To help prevent our fingers from being welded permanently to the glasses containing our cocktails, we were also issued with gloves. These were next to useless, however, when it came to the reclamation of our lips from their icy rims.

The clincher when it came to our decision to go for the VIP package was that you could have as many drinks as you wanted at no additional cost once you were inside the bar. I am not exactly a lightweight when it comes to the consumption of alcohol, so I was convinced that I could make this arrangement work out in my favour with minimal effort.

Placing our drinks onto tables made from ice without the aid of a coaster caused them to spin around like Torvill and Dean competing at an ice dancing championship and was our first mistake. The second was my refusal to wear my Cossack hat on account of its flattening effect on my hair. Underneath our fur coats, our clothes were geared to the searing temperatures outside and within ten minutes they were little defence against the biting cold creeping up our bare legs. Sitting on blocks of ice covered with only a thin faux animal skin was another factor in us realising that the offer of free drinks included in the VIP package was not as generous as it might have at first seemed. After only thirty-five minutes we were forced to exit the bar as the risk of hypothermia was becoming a distinct possibility and we had no wish to exchange the possibility of heatstroke with that of frostbite. We had managed to down only three cocktails in total making them anything but value for money. Like I said at the outset, Las Vegas is very much a place of contrasting realities.

Critical acclaim

Whether the speedy quaffing of cocktails in sub-zero temperatures has any effect on their potency, I am not qualified to know. What I do know, is that when we sat down to eat in a smart Thai restaurant, both Phil and I were certainly feeling the effects which, as we already know, can be the difference between the way I intend to behave as opposed to how I actually do behave.

Our fabulously camp server, who looked exactly like Liberace but without his trademark candelabra, began working us for a handsome tip, which was worth every penny on entertainment value alone. Figuring that it couldn't hurt our chances of making sure that the chef's attentions were similarly concentrated on our pleasure, I decided to tell Liberace that I was quite a well-known food critic back home in the UK. The colour visibly paled under Phil's tan as his expression communicated a phrase something along the lines of wtf? Liberace, though, was suitably impressed, especially when I cited Gordon Ramsay, who was quite big in the States at the time, as amongst the many famous chefs I had reviewed. Liberace took our orders, promising to alert the chef as to the presence of food royalty in his restaurant. Phil was positively hyperventilating at this point saying that I had probably put us both at risk of arrest for impersonating someone with the intention of gaining an advantage. I couldn't resist asking if he had forgotten to pack his sense of adventure, especially as it was the very reason I agreed to come on this trip in the first place. When Liberace returned with our food and a bottle of very expensive brandy with the compliments of the chef, Phil raised his beautifully cut crystal brandy balloon and said simply that what happens in Vegas should stay in Vegas.

Worth A Gamble

As a former businesswoman, I have spent a large chunk of my life narrowing the odds of success in my favour and, whilst I am not completely risk averse, I am certainly not inclined to leave things entirely to chance. Despite being in the casino capital of the world, I was more than content to live vicariously through others when it came to the act of gambling for so-called pleasure.

Whilst in the casino at the Venetian I even witnessed one guy lose an amount in the ballpark of $10,000 on the spin of a wheel, without batting so much as an eyelid. He seemed even slightly amused by my shocked reaction, telling me not to worry and that it was only money. My shock was not, as he seemed to think, because of any concern for his huge loss, but because I couldn't understand the stupidity of anyone throwing away that kind of money. It was even more troublesome to me when there were so many people outside on the strip hustling for just the tiniest fraction of that amount.

Phil, on the other hand, whose erstwhile errant sense of adventure seemed to be back on parade, was adamant that whilst we were in Vegas, we should sample all that it had to offer and that included a spot of gambling. Reluctantly, I agreed that I would join him for a class at Baby Gambling School, which was so named because it was for dummies like us who had no idea how to play any of the games typical to a casino. In a reciprocal gesture, he agreed to do something of my choosing after class that afternoon, although I told him nothing about my plans other than that they involved a bit of dressing up.

Trying to appear enthusiastic about spending the morning at Baby Gambling School, my spirits were slightly lifted when Phil and I were introduced to our teacher Hank, who was going to teach us the skills we needed to play craps. With his toned torso clearly visible under his pristine white shirt, I started to think that furthering my education might not have been such a bad idea after all.

Hank explained the rules and demonstrated how to throw the dice so that they hit the back of the table. Any player deemed to be not making a proper effort in this regard was at risk of having his bet voided. Like the good student, he was and after confirming that he understood the concept of inside and outside bets, something which still eluded me, Phil executed a successful throw. Cupping the dice in both hands, which I was promptly reminded by Hank was incorrect because the rules state you must use only one, I kissed my fist to add an extra theatrical flourish and launched my dice. Determined that my bet would not be voided because I hadn't made every effort to play off the back of the table, I threw the dice towards it as hard as I could. Unfortunately, this resulted in both dice clearing the table like two Olympic hurdlers, before landing on a game of blackjack behind it at a particularly tense point in the proceedings. Suitably unimpressed with what I had wrongly presumed was a reasonably subtle attempt to get expelled from class so that I could wait it out at the bar, Phil insisted that I keep trying until I perfected my technique. Despite graduating with my class, I am proud to say that I did not place a single real bet during my time in Vegas, which those of you familiar with this environment will appreciate was no mean achievement.

Not for the first time, Phil's tan paled to a colour resembling alabaster as we arrived outside the venue for my choice of activity for the afternoon. The exterior of the building we were about to enter was unambiguous as to its purpose and Phil followed me open-mouthed into one of the many quickie wedding chapels for which Las Vegas is famous. By now I could see that he was seriously concerned by this unexpected turn of events that had taken our *adventure* into truly unchartered territory. Taking him by the hand I welcomed him to our wedding and introduced him to Elvis who had been persuaded to re-enter the building specifically for this very special occasion.

Bemused Phil proceeded to shake Elvis by the hand as though everything that was happening was somehow within the realms of normal. I tried to make the most of my newly acquired skills learned at Baby Gambling School, but my ability to maintain a credible *poker face* was never destined to last more than a few minutes. Elvis filled two champagne flutes as I laughingly explained to Phil that the wedding was as fake as his sense of adventure, but hopefully not his sense of humour. We were there simply to dress up and try to convince our friends and family that we had indeed done the deed with a photographic record of the whole non-event. The look of sheer relief on his face was palpable as he knocked back his glass of champagne in a single gulp and then asked Elvis for a refill.

Helped by the calming effects of the pre-wedding drinks, Phil fully entered into the spirit of things from this point on. The Velcro strips on the back of my wedding gown could not be persuaded to meet so he placed his arm around me to hold the gown in place for the duration of the photographs, which added a further touch of authenticity. Phil even apologised for appearing to be so horrified by the thought that we were there for a real wedding and not a fake one. The effects of the wedding champagne caused him to add that he may even have gone through with it. Throughout the photo shoot, Elvis sang in the background as though he was in residence at Caeser's Palace, with his rendition of *Fools Rush in,* making me laugh out loud. Yes, sometimes I was undoubtedly a fool who often rushed in where no sane person ever would, but not even Phil's belated proposal of sorts or the effects of alcohol would have made me consider swapping my Vegas wedding for a real one. Maybe I was learning more on this impromptu *adventure* than I had ever expected to.

Immediately after our wedding, Phil suggested we might return to our hotel suite to consummate our marriage, to which I responded that I had been involved in enough fakery for one day. Instead, I set about sending out the photographic evidence of our nuptials with the hilarious responses making the investment of a few hundred dollars well worth the money. Only a very small number, and these were the people who probably know me better than I know myself, remained unconvinced by the apparent evidence of their own eyes.

In the middle of fielding the reactions to our afternoon escapade, the estate agent who was dealing with the sale of my house called to tell me that they had received an offer of the full asking price. I was thrilled to learn that the family home, that had stopped being that at the very moment Kenny died, had been sold at last. I sincerely hoped that another family might be able to bring our beautiful home back to life again and take advantage of the warmth and security we had always known under its roof. The flip side of this was, of course, that I needed to find somewhere else to live, which I had so far managed to avoid even thinking about. My buyers were not involved in any protracted chain and meant that the prospect of me becoming homeless shortly after my return to the UK was more likely than not.

The sale of my house was cause enough for a celebration, but as it was also my *wedding day* Phil and I cracked open another bottle of something from the minibar to mark this most momentous of occasions.

Once the bottle of something yet to be identified was drained to its base, I became convinced that I had reached the pinnacle of my decision-making superpowers. I deduced that the best way to deal with all the responsibilities that come with buying and selling a house was simply to ignore them. Before the effects of whatever was in the bottle I had been drinking from had the chance to wear off, I decided on direct action.

When I awoke the following morning with an inevitable hangover and just a handful of fuzzy memories from the day before, Phil obliged by filling in the blanks. I was to learn that after pressing a few buttons on a travel website, I now had exactly seven days after I returned home from Vegas to wash my unmentionables and re-pack them before flying back to the States, this time to the state of Florida. Somewhat less confident about my strategy of leaving all of the house selling/purchasing decisions to the last minute, I tried to cancel the trip but had already paid for it in full, with little chance of a refund.

My stomach reacted to the most recent pictures that had been added to the gallery on my phone by performing a summersault, which then caused a sick feeling deep inside it. I scrambled to recall the details of what I hoped was still a fake wedding and not something more permanent. Phil, of course, was unable to resist a retaliatory question concerning the shallow depths of my own sense of adventure, before reassuring me that neither of us had plighted our troth in any legally binding way.

Thanks to the combination of alcohol and the internet, I arrived back in the States seven days after I had left Las Vegas. Maybe the decision to flee to Florida had not been as random as it may have seemed, even to me. Once I was back on something I regard very much as home turf, I even toyed with the idea of driving down to Captiva Island. In the end, I was forced to accept that I didn't have the strength required to revisit a place which had meant so much to both Kenny and me. I did, however, spend my time retracing steps that we had walked side by side many times over, and, in doing so, found a peace I could not have found anywhere else on earth.

The morning that I arrived at the solicitor's office to sign the paperwork that would see me handing over our lovely home to another family, whilst purchasing another just for myself, was one of the most difficult things I have ever done. Not because I doubted the rationale of any of my decisions about the future, but because I knew that by acting on them, I was moving even further away from my past. As my pen hovered over the documents, I glanced at the empty chair beside me and felt Kenny's hand on top of mine guiding my signature, to show his approval of the direction I was about to take in the next stage in my life.

Phil and I went on to do our own thing, as we both always knew that in time we would. I strongly believe that some of the people you meet in life are never destined to be there for all of it, but are there when they are most needed. This was certainly true of Phil, who was exactly the right person to have an adventure with at a time when I had almost stopped believing in them. He helped to restore my self-confidence and reminded me that life is for the living and for this alone, he will always have a special place in my heart.

Chapter 8

Adrian

If Youth Knew; If Age Could – Sigmund Freud

I am including Adrian in this section of the book because there was a time when I considered him to be a serious contender to my *Ifs, Buts and Maybe's* category. Looking back now, I am baffled as to why, given what follows. I hope that by relating this experience here, it might provide a salutary reminder of just how easy it can be to ignore the basic rules of common sense, even for those of us who assumed we knew better.

Adrian made his initial approach through a dating site aimed at a middle-aged clientele and, in order to preserve the integrity of this aim, they did not accept anyone under the age of fifty. Bypassing this not-so-robust check was easily achieved, though, by providing a false date of birth on a membership application so that it would be accepted. This meant that the information in Adrian's profile showed him to be eight years my junior as a result. Whilst I didn't consider the age gap to be huge at the time, I did ponder briefly why a good-looking younger guy would show interest in an overweight, older but solvent widow. The answer, of course, was to be found somewhere within the question, but back then I had started to regard my healthy scepticism as the enemy of opportunity, that prevented me from exploring new and different options. Aside from this, there were very few clues as to the true nature of Adrian's agenda. Those that I did pick up on, supported the fact that it was probably financially motivated, but because this was an inconvenient truth at the time, I simply chose to ignore it.

Adrian's arrival on the dating site followed the discovery that his long-term and much younger partner had been cheating on him. She was also the mother of a son whom Adrian had come to regard as his own and was devastated when he was denied any ongoing contact after the split. This experience, he claimed, had scarred him to such an extent that he had no wish to become a father in the future under any circumstances. Had my sceptical tendencies not gone missing in action, I might have considered the possibility that Adrian was already laying down the groundwork to help reassure me that I had nothing to fear from investing my time in a younger man. His intention to remain childless certainly played into this narrative by addressing any fears a middle-aged woman might have about being replaced by a woman of childbearing age in the future.

It's good to talk

By the time I started talking to Adrian, which was often because once again there were some geographical challenges, I think my expectations were fairly minimal. In the same way that someone might consider a good night in, will include an episode of Strictly Come Dancing, complete with a glass of something in one hand and a Cadbury's crème egg in the other, I was happy to spend an evening curled up on the sofa with a drink and my laptop in that order of importance. Similarly, when the messages turned into phone calls, I was equally content to chat away until the early hours, all from the comfort of my own home. Whenever a face-time call was arranged, I ensured that my make-up was flawless and kept my phone focused on my face and not on the stained and sloppy pyjamas that I was usually dressed in out of shot.

Even now as I type this account of what transpired between myself and Adrian, I struggle to corral the words that describe the nature of these early communications. Our exchanges would range from those that were intellectually challenging to those that were sometimes disappointingly inane and boring. Adrian would, at times, come across as a man who harboured quite old-fashioned and chivalrous attitudes towards women whilst, at others, they were borderline misogynistic and dismissive.

What Adrian did not come clean about until some time later was that his lies concerning his age had been more extensive than he had led me to believe. During one telephone conversation, he suddenly announced that he had a confession to make. Implicit in the word confession is an acknowledgement of guilt, so I mentally ran through a list of the likeliest contenders. Perhaps he was going to confess to the existence of a wife after all, the fact that he was a wanted criminal or, even worse, a willing participant in military re-enactments at the weekends. When he admitted that he was actually fourteen years younger than I was and not eight as previously stated, this was something of a relief in the context of the possible alternatives. I probably should have bailed at this juncture, but as he had no doubt already calculated, Adrian was hoping that I was already sufficiently intrigued by him not to. His calculations will also have factored in the probability that I was extracting some enjoyment from being pursued by a good-looking much younger guy, finding it very flattering to the ego and in this he was not wrong.

His explanation for continuing to lie about his age was because he had started to really like me, he feared that had I known the truth I would have pulled away, which was also true. All of this sounded plausible, especially when told to someone as willing to believe it as I was.

Grief Blindness

There is no doubt that I took many unwise risks during the time I spent internet dating, but the true extent of the ease with which I dispensed with basic common sense was never more evident than during my dalliance with Adrian. As a consequence, this was probably the closest I came to being harmed emotionally, if not physically.

When conducting the post-mortem, after the demise of something that hardly qualified to be called a relationship, I struggled to find relevant explanations for my behaviour during it.

Having had many discussions over the years with members of GOWNS I identified a recurrent theme, which suggested that it was more common than even I had realised.

The term *widow brain* is one we are all familiar with and is used to describe the debilitating effects of the protective mechanism that shields a widow from the shock of their loss. Another widely accepted phenomenon is the tendency for bereaved spouses to become more susceptible to health problems as a result of the effect grief has on our immune systems. I contend that another lesser-known effect of grief on the brain should include those that are responsible for recognising and calculating risk. These effects are characterised by erratic decision-making and an inability to see the things that, prior to our loss, would have been obvious to us. I see examples of this in varying degrees in my contact with widows all the time and it is something I have started to refer to as *Grief Blindness.* The following is one such example that appeared on a forum for widows. It contains no identifying features but is a scenario I see replicated many times over.

Hello everybody

I am looking for advice, please. I lost my late husband two years ago and have been in a relationship with a man who lost his wife 10 years ago. Mostly he is kind and caring but after his wife died, he had another relationship with a lady who cheated and stole money from him and it has left him with trust issues.

I always try to let him know where I am and when I will be home so that he doesn't get anxious and annoyed when I am late back from shopping.

He doesn't like to socialise much and says that we have all we need in each other and even sulks when my grandchildren come to visit.

He doesn't work because he is on disability so I pay most of the bills and he moved into my house so that he could get some of the money back his previous partner stole. I don't mind helping him out but sometimes worry about my future as he has said he will never marry again. He has many good qualities and I know I should be grateful that I have found someone else to share my life with. Am I making something out of nothing here?

In my reply to this lady, I highlighted all the things that would have been of concern to me in her situation and which I imagine are obvious to all but this lady herself. My rule of thumb is that if you need to ask questions such as these of strangers, then it is highly likely you already know the answers. My point here is that *Grief Blindness* can seriously restrict your view of what would normally be blindingly obvious and the consequences can sometimes be quite devastating.

I am not a scientist and have no expertise that allows me to confirm whether my theorising has any basis in physiological fact. I am also happy to admit that the existence of *Grief Blindness* as a potential explanation for some of my own reckless behaviour, rather than that of rank stupidity, is also a far more palatable one. Whichever of these explanations you elect to believe is the root cause behind the disruption to the usual checks and balances that hold us all to account, the resultant effects are usually detrimental in varying degrees.

A Date With Death

Whether or not we are persuaded towards the existence of *Grief Blindness*, it is beyond doubt that drinking vodka from a pint glass does little to help the neurotransmitters in our brains that control our assessment of risk to work effectively. It was following one of these such assaults on what remained of mine that led to my meeting Adrian for the very first time.

Two years after losing Kenny I was to suffer the devastating loss of two of my dearest friends, who passed away on the same day at opposite ends of the country. My connection with each of these irreplaceable ladies had come about through our shared love of laughter and humour. I have absolutely no doubt that one of them would have found my plans for attending her funeral to be the stuff of comedy gold.

So it came to pass that on one sunny morning in early spring, I opened the front door of my home (where I was completely alone) to find Adrian standing on the step outside it. I gasped inwardly, as he was not at all what I had expected from the photos he had sent me. He looked older and less athletic and if he had any similar misgivings concerning his first impressions of the white-haired middle-aged lady who greeted him before welcoming him inside, he didn't show them. Because he had already driven for several hours in order to reach me, I had prepared some light refreshments to sustain us on the next leg of our journey, which was to be a long drive down towards the south coast.

It had never been my intention to attend my friend Catherine's funeral accompanied by anyone, but after I spoke to Adrian about my plans, he offered to lend his support and a shoulder to cry on if I needed one. Once again, his timing was spot on when it came to identifying the exhaustion that comes with creating an illusion of bravery. Losing both Catherine and Pauline so soon after losing Kenny meant that my reserves of bravado were heavily depleted, which made his offer both timely and appreciated.

Now, as I sat opposite this total stranger sharing lunch the enormity of what I had agreed to was beginning to land, this time without any of the cushioning effects of vodka. I did briefly consider faking a heart attack but ruled this out because I would likely miss Catherine's funeral altogether and give an incentive to certain members of my family to start the planning of mine. I also toyed with the idea of just coming clean and explaining to Adrian that I no longer thought it a good idea for him to come with me. In the end, I did absolutely nothing. Adrian insisted that he lift our overnight bags into the back of my car and I locked the front door behind us, effectively sealing my fate for the next forty-eight hours, presuming, of course, that I survived that long.

Alcohol Kills Weed Chills

The long journey down south gave us plenty of opportunity to talk and we both found enjoyment in the company of the other. Whatever the complexities of this man, he could be quite funny and entertaining and, by the time we reached our destination, I had high hopes that I might live to survive my stupidity after all.

On arrival at our hotel, once again Adrian chivalrously insisted that he carry the bags whilst I checked in and paid for the room, using my generous expense account. As Adrian was doing me a favour by being there, I certainly wasn't expecting him to be at a financial disadvantage because of it.

Later, when unpacking items from my overnight bag, I was annoyed to discover that I had forgotten my toothbrush and decided to head off out to the shops to buy one. Adrian wouldn't hear of it and said that I should stay in our room and relax after the long drive and offered to go to the shops himself. On his return sometime later, he had purchased not only one but three different types of toothbrushes for me to choose from, because he hadn't known which kind of bristle I preferred to use. I thanked him for his consideration as though he had just gifted me an expensive item of jewellery instead of a selection of toothbrushes purchased from the local Spa shop.

This brief closeness in proximity revealed that there was now an unmistakable aroma of weed present in the room that hadn't been there before. It seemed that concern for my dental hygiene was not the primary reason for Adrian's apparent willingness to take a trip to the shops. Realising that the pungent smell had not gone unnoticed, he quickly apologised if it bothered me. Looking towards the bottle of vodka from which I was now on my second measure, he explained that whilst some people liked to have a drink to help them relax, his recreational drug of choice was cannabis. In principle, I have no argument with this premise. The problem for me usually arises when people who use cannabis attempt to justify it as somehow intellectually superior to those of us who elect to get pissed on alcohol instead. Adrian was to prove no exception to this particular school of thought and decided that I needed to be educated on the error of my ways. He started by listing lots of ways in which alcohol is harmful and damaging to the body in ways that weed is not. I have had this conversation often enough in my life to be quite bored by it, to be honest. Yes there are many downsides to a reliance on alcohol, and I would not even try to argue a case against what are well established facts. Similarly, I saw no point in arguing that Marijuana can also have some fairly negative side effects, because in my experience those who use it are largely resistant to hearing them. Ultimately, it comes down to personal choice and, as the purpose of taking either cannabis or alcohol is to alter reality in some way, ultimately, the users of each are simply pursuing the same thing. Until whatever causes this need to escape from reality in the first place is resolved, we will continue to inflict damage on ourselves in varying degrees consistent with whatever our drug of choice may be.

Once this conversation was out of the way, Adrian dispensed with any pretence that his use of cannabis was anything other than quite extensive. This was evidenced by the various bits of paraphernalia that he was equipped with and would later also help to explain the paranoid tendencies that were yet to reveal themselves.

When we ventured out to a restaurant to have dinner that evening, which was only a short walk from our hotel to the restaurant, Adrian insisted that I stay closely by his side so that he could protect me in case of any trouble. About to make a wisecrack as to why anyone would want to cause harm to an old lady out for an evening stroll with her son, I thought better of it when I saw that Adrian was deadly serious. He started to scan both our surroundings and anyone passing by as though he was on a reconnaissance mission for the SAS.

Once inside the restaurant, if I thought Adrian might at last be able to let down his guard and relax then I was sadly mistaken. Instead, he was, keen to discuss the dangers faced by women alone, especially at night, saying he could tell by my relaxed manner that was I totally oblivious to them. I found this vaguely amusing as I looked around the restaurant at the other diners who were comprised mainly of young families, loved-up younger couples and older ones too where one half of them was not significantly older than the other. I explained that I was a long way from being blind to the risks faced by women in today's increasingly threatening society, but I have always been determined not to be restricted from living my life as I choose to because of them. I was left with the feeling that Adrian regarded me as some kind of poor innocent abroad, which is certainly not how I regard myself. After we finished eating, I settled the bill, before we headed back to the hotel. Once again, Adrian started to behave as though he was Kevin Costner charged with the task of protecting Whitney Houston.

Whilst waiting for the lift to take us up to our room, a group of lads entered the hotel to call a taxi to take them into town. Though harmless enough, it was obvious that they had already enjoyed more than a few scoops of the local brew. I responded to a bit of light-hearted banter and, when the lift arrived, a lady with a young toddler in a buggy struggled to manoeuvre her way out of it. On seeing that she was also wrestling with several other items of luggage, I reached out to give her a hand, along with the likely lads who also tried to help. Notably, the normally chivalrous Adrian made no attempt to offer his assistance. The little girl in the buggy started to cry and I asked her if she was ok. I don’t know why it happens that complete strangers seem to feel that they can open up to me, but it is not an irregular occurrence. The mother of the distressed little girl in the buggy started to explain that her daughter was probably crying because her daddy had left them both so he could go and f*** another woman. She added that she was probably hungry too, but the child's bastard of a father had left them with hardly any money to buy anything to eat, so she would have to wait until they got home, which was several hours' drive away. The likely lads did not hesitate to delve into their pockets and offered the poor woman all they had in loose change. I followed suit with an amount that was enough to ensure that both mother and daughter could get something decent to eat before their long drive home.

Implicit in his silence throughout this mini-drama, was Adrian's obvious disapproval which, once we were back in our room, he didn't hesitate to voice. He said that he was amazed to see that, despite his earlier warnings of stranger danger, I had still decided to engage with the lads waiting for their taxi in the lobby. I laughed and said that it had been nothing more than a playful exchange of harmless banter. Undeterred, he maintained that had it not been for his presence, this so-called innocent banter could have given them completely the wrong impression and escalated into something far more sinister and out of my control.

My response to this was that the type of guys who were willing to stump up a few quid to help a lady in distress were unlikely to be a threat to me or anyone else. Adrian shook his head in disbelief at what he called my incredible naivety, saying that the lady in the lift with the supposed marital problems probably used that same ruse several times a day. He said it was purely to extract money out of well-meaning strangers and that I was far too trusting for my own good.

On the face of it, some of what Adrian said might have had a ring of truth about it. I am inclined towards chatting with strangers and sometimes this could be said to be ill-advised. My instincts about people are usually good though and have kept me safe so far from any major harm. For reasons I couldn't quite put my finger on, I wasn't convinced that Adrian's claims of concern for my safety and welfare were what lay behind his apparent need to protect me, both from others, and myself. But for now, at least, I pushed these doubts to the back of my mind.

A Final Farewell

It was Catherine's wish that any tears at her funeral should be those associated with laughter and not sadness. We were asked to dress in ways that reflected our feelings for our dear departed friend, so I chose to wear white in honour of the wonderfully light and vibrant person that Catherine was, and because it sent a direct message to the darkness associated with death, which I know she would have appreciated.

As usual, however, I had paid little heed to the practicalities involved in creating the image I had hoped to cultivate on her behalf. Though it was early spring, the temperatures had plummeted to an almost glacial degree, making it necessary for me to cover my flimsy white apparel with a dark overcoat, so that my teeth didn't chatter throughout the proceedings. The beautiful woodland setting that Catherine had chosen for the last meeting place for all her friends and family also presented some logistical challenges. The car park was some considerable distance from the clearing in the woods where we were to sit on tree stumps to listen to the tributes from those who knew and loved her. This meant that the sparkly heels that I hoped would provide a final glamourous touch to my outfit were now similarly redundant, being no match for the uneven territory we were about to negotiate. I changed into some boots more suited to the task, and in doing so completed a look that had more in common with that of Sherpa Tenzing and rather less with the diaphanous vision in white I was hoping to create. I smiled to myself, wondering what Catherine would have made of the sight of me making my way through dense woodland terrain in clothing suitable for an assault on Everest, accompanied by someone who looked young enough to be her son. Had she also known that he was, in fact, a stranger to her until yesterday? My guess is that she would have been both bemused and somewhat amused by the behaviour of her unpredictable pal.

The memories of the gathering for Catherine's final farewell will remain with me always for lots of reasons. Poor Adrian, who had dressed in a smart suit for the occasion but had not brought an overcoat, was quite literally shaking from head to foot from the cold. Once the tributes were over and it was time to leave for the crematorium which would complete Catherine's final journey, he was desperate to get warm again. Even though I was wearing flat boots, with a fair wind behind us, walking back to the car at my pace was always going to leave him exposed to the cold for longer than he could bear. Instead, he suggested that he should run back for the car and then come back to pick me up, allowing him to thaw out and save me the effort of another trek through the woodland.

I handed over my car keys, happy with the very welcome benefits to myself as a result of this arrangement. As the other mourners gradually dispersed, it wasn't long before I was entirely alone in the middle of nowhere and the silence was like nothing I had ever experienced. At first, I used this solitude to spend a few moments thinking about Catherine, until other memories began to demand some space in my consciousness.

Back in the 1990's, during one of our early trips to Florida, Kenny and I had driven into a downtown area one evening to visit a well-known tourist attraction. Already familiar with valet parking we did not, however, expect to be stopped several streets away from the venue by a man motioning to us that we should give him our car keys in exchange for, what, he claimed, was a valet parking ticket. We did exactly as we were instructed, although we were both far from sure that we hadn't just handed our vehicle over to a random opportunist on the street and laughed at how easily we had surrendered our expensive rental car.

The obvious parallels with my current situation were not lost on me as the light started to fade rapidly now and there was still no sign of Adrian. I checked my phone but any glimmer of hope that I might have a signal was quickly dashed and meant I had no way to contact him, or anyone else for that matter. I don't know why I started to laugh out loud, because my situation was anything but funny, although it was most certainly laughable. I found myself having attended my friend's funeral in the middle of a forest in the back of beyond, that was becoming increasingly menacing now in the fading light. I had no phone signal and my only means of escape had possibly been stolen by a random guy I met through the internet. It is not a scenario that you could easily make up, and I can assure you dear reader that I have not.

Just as had been the case in Florida when our car was returned to us in exchange for what turned out to be a genuine valet parking ticket, Adrian also eventually reappeared with mine. The change in his demeanour was enough to explain the reason for his prolonged absence without him having to. I got into the driving seat and the unmistakable smell of weed permeated everything inside it, but my overwhelming sense of relief at seeing my car again made this seem unimportant by comparison.

If I wanted to be angry with Adrian once we arrived at the wake after the funeral, then I simply did not have the bandwidth to deal with that particular emotion. The sadness of Catherine's loss and the resultant resurgence of emotions associated with the death of my late husband was more than enough to bear. Resorting to a tried and tested method of dealing with the things I would rather not, I made several covert visits to the bar, which helped to make the world appear to be a less challenging place than it had before them. Perhaps sensing my earlier displeasure, Adrian neglected to deliver another lecture on the evils of demon drink and how unattractive he found drunken people. On the contrary, he even said he understood the need for me to drown my sorrows in the current circumstances.

Given that back then I needed little to no encouragement to drown anything I didn't like in alcohol, my recollections of the rest of the evening are not entirely complete. Those that did remain intact, suggest that Adrian and I had rather a pleasant evening and was at least one that I didn't have to spend alone, with only my memories for company.

After we arrived back at my house after the funeral, Adrian told me that, even though our first date had been far from conventional, he had enjoyed every moment. We had already made some tentative arrangements to meet up again the following month, but now he was saying that he didn't want to wait that long before seeing me again. He still had a long drive ahead of him, so said that he would phone me when he got home and to think about my availability in the meantime. I closed the door behind him and on possibly the most bizarre twenty-four hours of my life.

Gaslighting

According to one definition, the term Gaslighting is described as:

A manipulative tactic in which a person, to gain power and control of another individual, plants the seeds of uncertainty in another person's mind. The self-doubt and constant questioning slowly cause the individual to question their reality.

It is a form of coercive control and as such is currently regarded to be a criminal offence under the law in England and Wales. I recognise now that what I experienced with Adrian were his early attempts at exerting such control. They were quite subtle in nature, to begin with, but I am certain that they would have become far more forceful had I continued my *relationship* with him.

I didn't hear from Adrian later that evening after our return from the funeral, as he promised and not for several weeks after it. Initially, as I would have felt about anyone I knew who was facing a long drive alone in the dark, I was worried that he might have been involved in an accident. When he didn't reply to several of my messages asking him to contact me to let me know that he was okay I was forced to assume that he was either fatally injured or just full of shit.

If this was when my common sense should have returned from its lengthy vacation, I am ashamed to admit that it decided to book itself onto a world cruise instead. When Adrian did finally make contact with me again, his excuse for not doing so before was highly unlikely to have had even a smidgeon of truth to it. But, because there was a hugely emotive element to his explanation, I decided not to challenge him in favour of at least being seen to give him the benefit of the doubt.

We continued with our daily phone calls for a while, during which he would insist one minute that we make plans to see each other as soon as possible, only to cancel any arrangements within a matter of hours. I don't think I will ever know the true extent of his duplicity, but I strongly suspect that Adrian was engaged in several different *relationships* at the same time and that they were all probably in different stages of his manipulations of them. I was shocked by the extent to which I was prepared to engage with Adrian, especially when so many of the red flags that I would regularly teach others to recognise, were being waved right under my own nose and yet I still chose to ignore them.

I always imagined myself to be impervious to the manipulations of a romance fraudster, that my intellect and my instincts about people would prevent me from falling foul of their methods. What I learned was that I was vulnerable in ways I could never have imagined or considered possible. Having once thought I was strong not weak, smart not stupid and sensible rather than reckless, it never occurred to me that the loss of my husband could bring about such fundamental changes to the person I had been when he was alive. If I were to isolate all the first words paired in the sentences above, the words strong, smart and sensible were a reasonable summation of the person I used to be within the partnership of my marriage. Once I had been unceremoniously evicted from this part of my life, the words weak, stupid and reckless were far more applicable to describe the person I had become since.

Turning The Tables

I met with Adrian once more after Catherine's funeral and this time, without the sadness of her loss to negotiate, a lot of things came into far sharper focus. This time around it was much easier to identify his mood swings. His behaviours would oscillate between the kind and chivalrous version of him to then become those where he was barely able to disguise his impatience with me, which at times even bordered on contempt. This was a red flag I was not prepared to ignore and was something I suspected had the potential to become far more dangerous. During our last weekend together, I allowed Adrian to believe that I was the same gullible old lady he could be confident was still well and truly in his thrall.

I didn't even care that once again it was I who paid for us to eat out, for petrol and any of the other expenses that occurred during that last weekend. In fairness, Adrian did help me out with some things that I would have struggled to do alone without paying someone else to do them for me, so, in this respect, I regarded it as a fair exchange of resources. I suspected, however, that the plan was for this exchange to become less equitable in the future. In any event, I considered it a small price to pay for the lessons I learned and nearly didn't learn during my time with Adrian.

When Adrian left again after that weekend, I knew that I wouldn't see him again. I began to stop taking his calls and answering messages until he probably decided that I was no longer worthy of any further investment of his time or effort. This did not stop him from calling me in the early hours of one morning a couple of years later. I told him that I was happy in a relationship by then with a man who didn't care if I got drunk, or chatted with strangers. This was also a man who had no objection to me handing my own money to whoever I thought might need it and respected my ability to protect myself as much as he was willing to provide his, should I have needed it. Adrian listened before telling me that I had made my choice and that I would never hear from him again, though this was said in a manner that implied that he thought that I would live to regret my choice. To date, and for the first time in all my dealings with him, Adrian has stuck to his word and I haven't heard from him again. For my part, I have zero regrets about any of the choices I have made in my life since meeting him.

Chapter 9

The Truth About Fairytales

Twice Upon a Time

I started this book with an account of my wedding day in 1978, when I was just 18 years old. On the day I married Kenny it felt as though we were both living the stuff of fairytales. Boy meets girl, they fall head over heels in love and go on to live happily ever after. I have since learned that many of our favourite childhood fairy stories have their origins in tales that are quite sinister. The sanitised versions, that we are familiar with today, are the result of many rewrites throughout the centuries. These were then adapted by Walt Disney in his popular animated family-friendly films and became the basis on which his highly lucrative fairytale industry was built.

When I kissed a frog for the very first time, as I sat on the back of a rocking horse in a local park back in the 1970s, I knew then that he was no ordinary frog, but a prince among men. Having bought into the Disney version of what a happy ending should look like, I believed from that moment on that mine was all but assured. The truth, of course, is far less simplistic than that imagined by a young girl who had many reasons for wanting to exist in a fairytale. Behind the liberal sprinkling of Disney dust, however, some residual sinister overtones still persist in these tales of ancient origin and what she didn't know back then was that her happiness did not come without a cost.

Kenny may have been the first frog I ever kissed, but thanks to an ending written in poisoned ink by an unforeseen and malevolent force, he was never destined to be my last encounter with an amphibian. There were no circumstances ever, in which I could have envisioned myself puckering up in readiness to plant a snog on the lips of all the little f*****s who had joined a somewhat lengthy queue to enjoy one. Despite many attempts to persuade them otherwise, the majority of these pond dwellers steadfastly refused to commit to their inner prince.

If frog snogging wasn't how I expected to be occupying my time after losing Kenny, then getting married again was a prediction that I would not have made either. I can only assume that the evil bastards who had ballsed up my original happy ending had decided to give me another shot at one in recognition of all my endeavours in respect of the rehabilitation of frogs.

As I walked down the aisle for the second time on the 21st of September 2019 towards a man whose royal credentials were beyond reproach, I did so now with the full understanding that my future happiness came without any guarantee of a happy ending. We knew that our happiness had not been bestowed on us for free either and that living out a fairytale does not come cheap. Whatever the price of this one, it was a cost that we were both more than willing to pay.

The following is something I wrote for my website at www.sandraemanning.com a few weeks before I married my darling Craig, affectionately known to those who have read my first book, as the BHG (black hat guy).

The Funny Thing About Being a Widow 7 weeks and 1 day before your wedding?

Those of you familiar with the haphazard nature of the way I apply myself to matters of importance will not be surprised to learn that this fly-by-the-seat-of-my-pants attitude has not only failed to reduce them in size ahead of the wedding, but has also resulted in a distinct lack of planning for it too. So far, the venue is booked and I have designed (well I did a Moonpig type of thing) the invitations and sent them out only to be notified that the phone number provided for the RSVP has directed several of our guests to a Chinese takeaway instead of either Craig or my good self.

I have purchased several wedding dresses,all of which are currently taking up space in the filing cabinet in my office. Please don't take this to mean that I don't care about what sight will greet my new husband-to-be as I walk down the aisle. Once again, I have allowed my weight to creep back up and my reluctance to try on the tent-sized dresses which are my only options as a result, is a reflection of the disappointment I feel in myself.

Amid all things wedding, I have been working with a book cover designer in the US in preparation for the launch of The Funny Thing About Being a Widow? So time is a commodity in short supply at the moment. I am up at 4.30 am and usually in bed by 9.00 pm and the hours in-between seem to have much less than 60 minutes in each of them as a result, I now have several, back-to-back episodes of Four in a Bed to catch up on.

As I contemplate the up-and-coming changes in my life, I can barely believe my luck. Kenny died on the 12th of August 2014 after which I developed my cunning plan, something I describe in my book in some detail but for now, I will simply say that it is a very good job that it didn't work.

I know how fortunate I am to be spending my days doing what I love to do and learning new things as I do it. On top of this, I have met, and am about to marry, a truly wonderful man who I love with all my heart. Never a day goes by where I am not thankful for the life that I once had and I hope that Kenny is proud of my attempts to honour each of his three requests, but I am also beyond grateful for the life I am living now too.

Crikey, is that the time? I feel I really should be making an effort to order something wedding-related from Amazon but am struggling with what exactly this should be. I seem to be suffering from a resurgence of the condition that is cash incontinence and is characterised by spending lots of money on stuff I neither want nor need.

Currently, I am awaiting the delivery of a bump. This is a device that will make the significant amount of hair I already have look even fuller. Quite what I do with it once it has been bumped, however, is somewhat less clear.

On a more practical level, I also need to purchase some scaffolding from Simply Be to wear under whichever of the final three dresses make it out of my filing cabinet. I perhaps should delete the JUST EAT app on my phone with 7 weeks and 1 day to go to the wedding and replace it with the Weight Watchers one instead. I am not holding my breath, though, at least not until the wedding photographs, when I will be sucking it in to the point of becoming puce.

The seven weeks and one day that followed the writing of this blog flew by incredibly quickly. As I get older, I am aware that the passage of time does so at a much speedier rate of knots than it appeared to when I was a younger person. My dear departed mother, whose life had been so restricted by illness, would often warn me that time was precious and I should use it wisely because as we get older it suddenly acquires the legs to outrun what is left of your ambitions. I had forgotten this until I wrote the sentence above and realised that I had now reached the point in my own life where I could fully appreciate what she meant.

The following is a blog I wrote about the concept of time for my blog at www.sandraemanning.com I like to remind myself of its contents whenever I find myself wasting the time I have left, when I should be living in appreciation of every moment of it.

A Question Of Time

Oookay people...I have been reflecting on the construct that is time this week, a commodity we consider ourselves not to have enough of, or conversely, is also something that can drag interminably too.

What of the world before the division of time? Of course, natural divisions have always existed. In most parts of the world, night follows day and the seasons dictate when we reap and sow, and when animals migrate or mate. But it was the ancient Babylonians who gave us hours and the Greek astronomers who further simplified their system of sixty, into minutes and seconds.

Time elapses, according to the same measure, every twenty-four hours, it never varies so why then do we say things like time flies? Is this phrase ever used by those accommodated within the walls of HMPS or does the life of an old lag drag whilst they do their time? Why is it that we can't wait for stuff to arrive, or for certain things to happen when we know we have no choice but to wait for either?

We are inclined to complain if our food arrives late to our table in a restaurant (in the days when it wasn't just Salmonella you were risking by attending one) but if the food arrived too soon, we immediately suspect the involvement of a microwave and refuse to eat it.

Why do we bother with timetables for trains and buses when everyone knows they are always late and smell worse than socks that haven't been washed for an extended period of time? Aeroplanes always miss their time slot on an outward journey, but are usually piloted by the air-born equivalent of Lewis Hamilton on the way back to defy the clock and get you home almost before you set off in the first place.

Time can even assume a persona in its own right when described as being lovely or hard, as in Charles Dickens' The Best of Times and The Worst of Times.

You can spend time however you wish and oh, boy, how we covet our free time, but is time ever free? From the cradle to the grave, the way we spend it is mapped out by the expectations of society. Today's children no longer 'Watch With Mother' because they are usually shipped off to nursery instead. This allows mum and dad to get back to work, which in turn makes them appreciate their free time when it comes as the result of being off work. The nursery owners who profit from this arrangement are pretty appreciative of this approach to time management too. Education and then employment continue to gobble up precious minutes, hours and years and whilst we strive for financial security (at least those of us who still like to wash occasionally and don't spend their time protesting during a pandemic) time marches relentlessly on.

Isaac Newton's contention that we are merely occupying time makes a lot of sense to me. I know that at 60 years old and slowly making my way towards the departure lounge of life's journey, I am more conscious than ever that by whatever measure of time I choose to use, whether it be a sundial or a Fitbit, I won't need either indefinitely as retirement approaches.

My current preoccupation with time has, ironically, meant that I got to spend some more of it in contemplation of the way I have expended this valuable commodity thus far. I have, as a result, and to use another time-honoured phrase, found myself wishing in some ways that I could have my time all over again.

By this, I don't mean I regret the ways in which my life turned out, at my age now, though, and with the benefit of the hindsight that this brings, I might have made an effort to allocate a little more time for myself. As I approach retirement maybe that type of quality time will prove to be the icing on the cake of this particular slice of my life. I might actually enjoy having time on my hands if I can ignore the fact that the latter years bring physical challenges of their own.

The loss of my 20/20 vision, for instance, means that I have trouble reading Google, which has become an essential aid to the increasing lapses in my memory in its own right. I haven't asked it yet for the reason I have walked into a room but it's getting close.

I have never conformed to a timetable in my entire life and although I am usually punctual I am guilty at times of being reactive rather than proactive. So today I have produced a timetable in the hope that it will help me to focus on the things I still hope to achieve in whatever time is still mine to spend.

As I look at my timetable with its neat columns that divide my time in ways that quite frankly might be impossible to follow unless I learn to say the word 'no' in several languages, I feel excited and nervous. Excited because I have never been organised and can see how the timetable will undoubtedly improve my rate of productivity, but nervous because this bloody sheet of A4 has the power to change me too.

I'm not sure if I will like a super-efficient version of myself or, more to the point, will anyone else? I might become obsessed with time management and go back to eating foods with only P's and Z's in their name as a way of saving time cooking. Add the effects of a diet like this to the lockdown pounds I have already acquired, this will probably mean that I will need to order a mobility scooter to get around. Christ, they only go 6mph; how much time will that waste?

Blimey, is that the time, folks? I would love to stay and chat, but my timetable has other plans for me. I am allowed a vodka break in about an hour and if I chuck them down quickly enough, I might summon up enough Dutch courage to wipe my arse with the timetable shortly thereafter!

I wrote the next blog for my website at www.sandraemanning.com several weeks after I married Craig, where anyone wishing to can see photographs of our big day.

To make use of a tennis analogy, it is important now that I find myself playing in the final set to go for every single shot until I hear the words Game Set and Match, regardless of whether or not I emerge as the winner.

The Wedding Blog

Some weeks have now passed since the day of our wonderful wedding and Craig and I have both finally arrived at a place of reflection. There is no doubt that, because we are both of a more mature vintage than your average bride and groom, excitement of this magnitude has proved to be more than a little exhausting. However, whilst the benefits of having more years behind you than in front of you may not seem immediately obvious, it does at least mean that our advancing years have taught us how to savour each and every precious moment as they present themselves.

Both Craig and I got exactly the kind of day that we hoped for, which probably owed a lot to the haphazard way in which it was planned, if indeed any real planning was involved at all. During the months before the wedding, we were frequently assured that a high level of stress is all but compulsory when organising an event such as a wedding. However, those of you who know me already understand that urgency is not my thing. I prefer to spring into action only at the point when ignoring what needs to be done is no longer a viable option.

When you add to this the fact that I have two of the most organised people on the planet amongst my nearest and dearest there was never any need for us to stress out, to use a somewhat overused and modern-day term.

During the few conversations that did take place concerning our expectations of the wedding, our contributions tended to be an articulation of the things we didn't want rather than those we did.

Questions concerning the top table and who should be sitting at it were met by a decision that we should dispense with one altogether. At our ages friends and family are fewer than they once were and we saw no point in pissing off those we had left by seating them somewhere that might lead them to question their order of importance in our lives. The existence of a dress code was similarly dealt with. Whilst we appreciated the sentiment behind wedding party members wishing to avoid anything that might clash with the bride, it really wasn't an issue for me. I wasn't aiming for the cover of Vogue and didn't think for a moment that there would be any conflict of image when it came to an overweight sixty-year-old bride, which would have excluded any potential clashes on those grounds alone.

Oddly enough we did arrive at a colour scheme of sorts, although this only happened as a result of a few bottles of pre-wedding Chablis. The wine was instrumental in helping to convince us that our ideas in this respect were nothing short of inspired. We decided that Craig's son Jack and my two grandsons should all look as though they had just walked off the set of a Blues Brothers film. Towards this end, they wore Navy suits accessorised with trilby hats and sunglasses whilst on their feet they wore wonderful navy blue patent winkle picker shoes. I can only imagine how they might have looked should we have chosen to drink something stronger than wine during our one and only attempt at making any kind of plan for the wedding.

My final choice of wedding dress came from one of the three that I had been storing in a filing cabinet in my office for some months prior to the wedding, mainly because it was also Navy blue and the only one that fit. In all honesty, the dress didn't matter and I would happily have worn a bin liner as long as Craig and I ended the day as the new family we were hoping to become.

Let them eat cake, so the saying goes, but who the heck ever eats any of the wedding cake, which is another part of the ritual of marriage? Unable to deal with the howls of protest when we suggested that we felt no particular need to adhere to this particular tradition either, I gave in and bought a plain one from M&S and decorated it myself, purely to satisfy the obligatory wedding photo opportunity.

Once we had established our list of all the things we didn't want, our wish list containing everything that was important to us both was all present and correct on the day itself. It was wonderful to see the faces of those who, because life gets in the way sometimes, we don't see as often as we would like. Even now, some weeks later, I can still feel my sister's touch as she wrapped her arm tightly around my own and led me towards the man who would become my husband. This simple embrace spoke volumes about her support for the new life that I was about to step into, as it was also confirmation of the importance of everything that had preceded this moment.

My sister and I proceeded down the aisle to a completely different song from the one I had chosen, due to an error on the part of the wedding planner. She was horrified and couldn't understand why I was not, but I already knew that even the best-laid plans are often subject to change without notice.

Gripping each other's hands tightly, Craig and I managed to exchange our vows without shedding a tear despite several close calls. This was not true, though, for many of those bearing witness to our nuptials, who were crying not just because they were happy for us but for some of them this was an event that also served as a reminder of what we had lost too.

When it came to signing the register, I reached out for my glasses, without which I couldn't have seen to order a takeaway let alone sign a legal document and I noticed that Jack (Craig's son) was sobbing uncontrollably. Fearing that the reason for his tears might have been because he saw our marriage as the point at which he was somehow losing the father he adores, I was sad that I couldn't provide him with reassurances to the contrary. Once I was able to extend a comforting arm around him, he told me that the real reason for his tears was because of the pain in his feet, not his heart. The fabulous blue patent winkle picker shoes that Craig and I insisted that all the boys wore to complete their outfits had all gotten mixed up when they had been getting dressed for the ceremony. As a consequence, Jack was wearing a pair several sizes too small which had crippled him to the point of tears and also explained why my grandsons had been walking around like two Emperor penguins during their entrance as well.

As I look back now on the ingredients of an imperfectly perfect day, during which Craig and I gave ourselves each to the other and created a host of precious memories that will last throughout both of our lifetimes and beyond, I know that we could not have planned it better.

I would like to dedicate this blog to my favourite Aunty Beryl who passed away whilst Craig and I were on our honeymoon. She was 88 years old and was always a huge inspiration to me and faced life with both fortitude and bravery. I will especially remember her as having an infectious sense of humour and for her fierce love of her family. I will miss her always xxxxxxx

A Basket Case

To be honest, I was sulking at Craig's suggestion of activity on the second day of our honeymoon, but more of that later. Again, consistent with the arrangements for our wedding, the inclusion of a holiday after it was last minute. Don't get me wrong, we both love our holidays, but tend to take them on a fairly ad-hoc basis. Though we didn't feel any particular need to conform to the tradition that is a honeymoon, we booked one anyway, again more to appease the expectations of others than any of our own.

We chose the destination for our honeymoon with the help of a pin and a map. Also because it was a place I had often heard described as beautiful in many of the conversations I had endured concerning holidays during my years as a hairstylist.

Due to the last-minute nature of our booking, Craig and I arrived at the airport to find that we had been allocated seats at totally different ends of the aircraft. I resorted to the use of emotional blackmail to rectify this and alerted the lady at the check-in desk that we were newlyweds, before adding that at our ages it was by no means certain that we would live long enough to reach Madeira, let alone survive the rigours of a honeymoon. If this was to be our last sojourn then it would be amazing if we could experience it sitting in seats that were next to each other. This pathetic ploy proved successful on the outward-bound flight but was met by zero interest when I tried a similar tactic to blag us seats together on the plane bringing us home.

We arrived In Madeira and I was struck immediately by both its beauty and the fact that most of it was built on a mountain. Given that I have been known to experience a nosebleed on anything higher than a doorstep, and even purchased a house that I thought was a bungalow so that I could avoid stairs, this was not an especially welcome discovery.

The hotel was beautiful though and the spectacular dining room, which overlooked a harbour hosting the most magnificent of cruise ships, could be viewed through a wall of floor-to-ceiling glass. When Craig and I went down for breakfast on the first morning of our trip, the sun was already streaming in through the windows and the ocean outside glittered as though it were a carpet comprised of diamonds. Most of the other diners had chosen seating in a shaded area, but I was so enthralled with the dazzling view, that I persuaded Craig to join me at a table in the brighter half of the dining room. The food didn't disappoint and I was particularly impressed to see that the wonderful breakfast buffet included bottles of sparkling wine in buckets of ice. As it was our honeymoon, and probably even if it hadn't been, we happily indulged ourselves in several glasses.

The cooling effects of the chilled sparkling wine did little to combat the greenhouse effect of the sun on the glass or the blinding light coming from the sparkling sea. Within minutes both Craig and I were sweating like two hogs on a spit and couldn't see two feet in front of our noses. Although I couldn't actually see them, the sense of smugness that exuded from the diners who had chosen seats in the shaded half of the dining room was palpable.

Craig suggested that we move tables, but, for reasons I don't always understand about myself, my need to outsit the smug bastards sitting in the shade was far stronger than my desire to see again or to register a normal temperature. Trying hard to please his new wife, Craig sat it out with me and we managed to finish our food. Scrambled eggs with smoked salmon and sweat are an acquired taste but aren't nearly as bad as they sound. During the process of trying to contain my eyeliner with a wet wipe, I recovered my sight sufficiently to see that my husband, a man with several known cardiac issues, was experiencing a significant level of discomfort. Fearing that this had reached the point at which he would need to be carted off to the hospital with heatstroke, we slid quietly off our chairs and returned to the air-conditioned confines of our hotel room.

Once recovered, my husband was soon planning our activities for the day. I, on the other hand, had one eye on the pool and a sun lounger, with the other one focused firmly on the ice buckets containing more sparkling wine on the bar at the side of it. I froze inwardly at the mention of cable cars, recalling a wet and windy day in Llandudno when, as a child, I had been forced to travel up the Great Orme in one that swung about like a pendulum on speed. If this wasn't bad enough, my husband also thought it might be fun to travel back down the mountain in nothing more substantial than a wicker basket, whose braking mechanism relied on the feet of two guys behind pushing it. The excited look on his face as he tried to sell this activity to someone who quite frankly would have preferred to have eaten her own face, prevented me from refusing to go or feigning a serious illness. I opted in favour of a silent sulk and followed Craig as he dragged me to a bus station, which in itself, did little to lighten my mood, which would then take us to the cable cars.

I have to admit that the scenery, once we began our ascent whilst dangling perilously from a wire that looked no stronger than string, was absolutely glorious. I allowed one corner of my mouth to turn slightly upwards momentarily, although the thought of what was still to come was enough to bring it firmly back into sulking position tout suite.

I am not usually lacking in adventurous spirit and I only had myself to blame for my distinct lack of it now. Failing to heed the lessons concerning the effects of complacency on my eating habits, and then subsequently on my shape, I had allowed my pre-dating site physique to make something of a comeback. The prospect of cramming all these added extras into the confines of a flimsy wooden vehicle, to then hurtle down a hill in it, was not filling me with the same sense of excitement that Craig was clearly experiencing. I consoled myself with the fact that we would at least be travelling downhill and not up it. When the time came for us to clamber aboard a basket, I tried to choose one driven by basket pushers who appeared to have plenty of rubber left on the soles of their shoes.

The corners of both sides of my mouth reacted in an upward motion during our speedy and twisty descent, this time without any attempt from me to try and stop them. Once we were back at base camp, I was thrilled that I hadn't let my size prevent me from having this experience, although in truth, had it not been for Craig, I probably would not have chosen it for myself. I took a few moments to take a few deep breaths and appreciate how very lucky I was to be enjoying life again which I owed in no small part to my presence on a dating site and the click of a mouse at precisely the right moment. I know that dating sites are not for everyone, but with a little perseverance and persistence they can and do work for some people. Anything in life that is worth having will require effort to achieve it, and I am beyond grateful that Craig decided that we were both more than worthy of such an effort.

Chapter 10

Life Post Dating Sites – The Results

Covid-19

Once the wedding we didn't plan and the honeymoon we didn't think we needed were over, the world was about to change in ways we could have never predicted. The arrival of COVID-19 on our shores brought with it an all too familiar sense of foreboding as my childhood and much of my life as an adult had been dominated by my mother's health issues. When I lost Kenny, I vowed to make the most of a life that no longer had the spectre of ill health and death central to its core. As per usual though, fate had other plans in store for me when it decreed that I would meet Craig under a black hat on a dating site. He was honest with me from the get-go concerning his own significant health issues and, whilst I admired his honesty, I admit to some doubts about becoming involved with someone who faced so many uncertainties. In the end, any doubts were overridden by my feelings for a man whose seemingly limitless supply of positive energy and resilience made it impossible not to fall in love with him. Even now he repeatedly tells me that he is *invincible,* which I used to think was just plain silly. Now I am not so sure that he isn't, as he continues to repel each threat to his health as though he was doing no more than swatting away an irritating insect.

Of course, in the early days of the pandemic, with no effective treatments available and the development of a vaccine still some way off, I was petrified that if Craig were to catch this dreadful virus it would be a death sentence for him, as it proved to be for so many others.

The lockdown, when it came, was something of a relief to be honest, although I do understand the political arguments made against it, some of which came with the benefit of hindsight. Any policy that would help reduce Craig's potential exposure to COVID seemed like an eminently sensible one to me and, in any event, was the only course of preventative action that was available to us at the time.

I suppose, like most people, I didn't think that this brutal interruption to our lives would last as long as it did, and the early days of lockdown were something of a learning curve. When we discovered that the ramparts, pulled up for our protection, could be lowered to accommodate a supermarket delivery we quickly adopted a type of bunker mentality.

As a teenager growing up in the 1970s, I can vividly recall the miner's strike which had forced the government of the day to ration electricity for three days every week. During these days we were plunged into darkness and forced to function in candlelight. We had to manage without the three TV channels that we did have access to, although we could still listen to our battery-powered radios. Back then there was no such thing as the internet, or the multiple devices that connect to it that are now part of our everyday lives and without which we now struggle to function. Far from being disturbed by any of the effects on our lives brought on by the imposition of a three-day week, I remember that if anything we were quite excited by it. Being holed up now in our comfortable home with Netflix to keep us entertained and a steady supply of food and alcohol brought to our front door, lockdown didn't seem to be all that much of a sacrifice either at the time. It certainly didn't equate with any of the horrors faced by previous generations, who had been called upon to fight and die for their country en masse.

However, this laissez-faire attitude was born out of ignorance of the effects that locking people down in their homes would come to have on them in both the short and longer term. When the schools closed, I found myself as a new stepmother, educating Craig's son Jack at home, as lots of us did. This inevitably meant that the projects I had hoped to work on, that were commensurate with the future that Craig and I planned for us all as a family, were put on temporary hold. As I tried hard to plug the holes that were left by the withdrawal of Jack's education in the best way I could, the restrictions started to bite. Craig and I are both from a generation that was taught to face adversity with a stiff upper lip and believe that what doesn't kill you makes you stronger. There is no doubt, however, that we both found that the lockdown restrictions affected us more than we were ever likely to admit to anyone except each other.

As the days turned into weeks and months, our cosy bunker started to feel less and less comfortable and more like a prison in which the walls were moving ever closer together. Having negotiated the vagaries of internet dating and finding each other, Craig and I became increasingly frustrated by the impositions placed on us by the pandemic. Just because we were older than the average newlywed couple did not mean that we hadn't thought about, and planned, a future that was based on the availability of time that was now being taken away from us. At this stage of our lives, it was more important to us than ever to enjoy as many adventures as possible whilst we were still physically able to have them. I am fully aware that, by comparison, our experience of lockdown was not as bad as it was for a lot of people, but this knowledge did little to diminish our sense of frustration at the time.

The following is a blog I wrote for my website on www.sandraemanning.com as the lockdowns began to lift. It was another attempt at dealing with a subject that is far from funny, but need not be devoid of humour nonetheless. The effects of lockdown for me, personally, were more far-reaching than I could have imagined and those effects are something I still struggle with to this day.

When Springs Are Bustin' Out All Over

Today I feel the need to talk about my humble armchair, which until very recently was pretty much my permanent place of residence. Now, after performing that particular function in a manner that was over and above the call of duty for almost two years, my lockdown chair, has not unreasonably, decided to call time on its relationship with my bottom.

I always knew that this parting of ways was both inevitable and necessary at some point, but remained largely ignorant of the unhealthy nature of our relationship until the time I was forced to acknowledge that it was finally over.

Such was the level of comfort provided by my armchair that I was seldom tempted to leave it, notwithstanding toilet breaks or a walk along the hallway to take delivery of a takeaway meal and call it exercise. However, once I ventured outside again, specifically to select a replacement on which to park my newly expanded posterior, I started to discover the full extent of the negative consequences that come with a chair-dwelling lifestyle.

Having had no need of normal footwear for so long, I discovered that when I did try to force my feet into my shoes, the square peg and round hole was a good analogy to describe how it felt. The generosity of my lockdown slippers had allowed my feet, which now bore a startling resemblance to two meat puddings, to spread into their expandable space without restriction. If I thought that the act of simply standing up, something I had come to consider as part of my exercise regime, would be enough to convince them to shrink back to their former size then I was sadly mistaken.

Similarly, my clothes, like my confidence, seemed to have shrunk since I last had any need of these either and pyjamas, like slippers, are excellent at providing room for expansion. At first, I blamed the tumble drier for shrinking my clothes, despite knowing that since I had taken to living in my nightwear its services had rarely been required. The truth of it was that my own greed and gluttony had been responsible for rendering my entire wardrobe redundant. Not for the first time, I had to resort to ordering replacements from an online plus-size clothing company. I was heartbroken that I needed to patronise it again after losing a significant amount of weight in order to join several dating sites, one of which led me to my wonderful husband.

I had retained nothing worth remembering concerning the effects of complacency on my waistline. Without protest, I willingly allowed platefuls of Pizza to sneak up behind me and attach their substantial calorie count to my hips, just as they had done so successfully during my first marriage. Pizza is thought of as a convenient and tasty food choice for families, but its effects on sedentary married women are both under-researched and misunderstood. Because my arse was permanently parked in my armchair for two years, my new husband was unable to see the true extent of the damage caused by this stealthy Italian staple until it was far too late to warn me.

The demise of any relationship is usually characterised by the negotiation of certain stages, which for me started with feelings of anger. By representing itself as a place of support and sanctuary during COVID, my trusty armchair was in fact not acting in my best interests at all. It became my dining room and my home cinema, encouraging my profligate use of Netflix and occasionally even doubling up as my sleeping quarters when I had one too many of the aperitifs that I kept within easy reach by its side. In short, this charlatan aided and abetted all my excesses without any consideration of the long-term effects of facilitating this level of indulgence.

I fully appreciate that lots of people were able to maintain perfectly healthy relationships with their furniture during the pandemic. In huge numbers, they took to walking, cycling and many other forms of exercise which had undisputed benefits, not only for themselves, but also provided a welcome respite for their lockdown armchairs.

My armchair came from a charity shop, which I now understand may have predisposed it towards charitable intentions. By indulging my every whim in gratitude for me giving it a home in which to see out its final days, I can only presume it didn't realise that our mutual appreciation of each other would lead us both into an unhealthily co-dependent relationship as a result.

So now we have arrived at the next stage of our breakup, which is a place of forgiveness. The comfortable cushions that were perfectly positioned for plates, pint pots and even wet wipes for washing, so I didn't even need to leave it for this either, were all offered from a place of charitable intent and not one of intentional harm.

I have feelings of enormous guilt that it took the suicide of the springs beneath the upholstery of my trusty companion to force me into contemplation of a return to a world I was increasingly content to live without. Whilst I don't want the sacrifice of my armchair to have been made in vain, I am not sure that I can learn to walk normally again or reduce those heinous numbers on the size labels of my clothing. Perhaps more to the point, I am not sure I am interested in even trying.

I find myself, therefore, at something of a crossroads. One road will lead me towards another armchair, so that I can carry on living vicariously through Netflix, whilst another fork offers me a return route to the resumption of a life forever changed, though thankfully not ended by COVID.

Ultimately, whichever path I choose, the purchase of a replacement armchair was necessary, if only for practical reasons and already it seems that my current choice is significantly less welcoming than its predecessor. This, of course, could prove to be a mere figment of my imagination and confirmation that these decisions are actually all within my own purview. If I am at least ready to re-enter the world's atmosphere, learning to stand on my own two feet puddings again, may not be as simple as it sounds. My confidence was deeply affected by life in lockdown and I was unwisely quite blasé about my decision to allow it to leave the building unchallenged. Now I find myself feeling its loss in the same way that I would miss the functions carried out by one of my limbs and appreciate how much easier life was when I could rely on it without question. It is my dearest hope that, as I seek to reunite myself with my former level of confidence, it also enjoyed the benefit of having somewhere comfortable to sit during the wait.

This post is dedicated to a very loyal armchair...RIP old friend, I miss you and will try hard not to put upon your successor in the same way. You might also be pleased to know that I lost 3Lbs this week and have sworn off Pizza at least for lent, if not for life.

Is There Anybody There?

If I thought that when I emerged from lockdown, I would feel like a kid let loose in a sweetshop with an unlimited budget, then this was a long way from how I actually felt. I have never suffered from agoraphobia in my life. If anything I tend to feel claustrophobic in confined spaces and panic if I don't have easy access to my car whenever I feel the need to escape something that seems even slightly restrictive. There was no doubting it now, though, that after two years without the kind of stimulation that I had become accustomed to in my life before COVID, things had changed dramatically.

Whilst I was fine to take car journeys that were on local routes and with which I was familiar, I no longer had any desire to proceed further. Having been someone who would regularly travel the length and breadth of the country without a second thought, this was previously unheard of. Knowing that I was finally free, but for reasons I could not fully comprehend wasn't able to take advantage of it in any appreciable way, was beyond frustrating. Similarly, now that we were allowed to eat out for no other reason than we were hungry and not because we wanted to *help out* the government, I found that I didn't want to do this either. The Just Eat app on my phone, which required me to do nothing more than Just That, as far as I was concerned, was a winning formula that I could discern no tangible benefits from tampering with.

Perhaps the biggest surprise of all the changes in me as a person, was my post-COVID change in attitude towards travel. Under normal circumstances, I have never needed more than a few seconds to be persuaded into packing a bag and pissing off pronto in search of pastures new. Not anymore, now I had turned into a staunch advocate of the staycation, a phrase that became part of our language during lockdown and which I interpreted in the most literal way possible.

Keeping any movement in my major muscle groups to a bare minimum, I would search for images of my favourite Captiva beach online. Then I would cast them to my seventy-five-inch TV whilst playing the sound of the ocean, courtesy of YouTube. By opening a few windows, I was able to create the equivalent of a sea breeze in my own living room. After a trip to the fridge to get a refreshing cocktail, I had every ingredient I needed to enjoy a virtual vacation without any of the hassle of airport delays.

I will admit that of all the changes I experienced to my normally exuberant zest for life in general, this was the one that upset me the most. If these changes to who I was bothered me, Craig must have wondered if the person that he had married not so long before had ever existed at all. Being the resilient character that he is, my darling husband negotiated his re-emergence into the world with nothing but gratitude for the opportunity to do so. I, on the other hand, remained fearful of finding any vestiges of the person I used to be.

Other Changes

When I moved to the Doll's House, which readers familiar with the contents of my first book might recall turned out to be a house and not the bungalow that I wrongly assumed it was, it was always my intention that my tenure here would be short and sweet. From the point of purchase, my instincts were already telling me that this was not where my story would end. I felt that there would be more chapters yet to come in the story of my life, and there was at least one more adventure waiting in the wings to be written about. Having already enjoyed the rural location of my previous family home, I hoped that my next move might be to somewhere close to the sea.

These vague plans, however, had not taken into account the effects on them of a chance meeting on a dating site with a man who would become my husband. For his part, having already lived by the coast, Craig was soon on board with my plans to relocate, not only to somewhere by the sea, but perhaps to somewhere with a warmer climate and a different culture. Not for the first time in both our lives, fate had other plans.

So that we could give Jack every opportunity to repair the damage done to his education by COVID, we put our plans on hold so that he could attend a good school. This required us to remain at the Doll's House in the short term and to make it into a home that reflected the things that were important to both of us.

On this basis first up was the installation of a bar. If a trip down to the local pub was still not something that held any particular appeal for me, the solution was to bring the experience closer to home. My wonderfully talented husband, who can make anything out of nothing, set about creating a bar in our garden. This meant that we could enjoy all the amenities of our favourite local only a few short strides away from the Doll's House. Given the looming cost of living crisis, which was to follow COVID, this also turned out to be a prudent investment.

Wispa

Craig and I are both dog lovers, having owned one throughout most of our respective lives. Because we had been expecting to relocate, and possibly to somewhere abroad, we resisted the very real temptation to find a dog until things were more settled. Now that our plans had changed and before we set about refurbishing the rest of the Doll's House, we decided to go ahead and get a puppy. It was as good a time as any to absorb the inevitable damage done to furniture, that we intended to replace anyway, caused by tiny puppy teeth.

The search for our lovely chocolate labrador, who we called Wispa, took us to a farm in South Wales and from there we brought her home to begin her new life and enrich ours in ways that are not easy to articulate, even for me.

As Craig and I started to gather together all the different elements that reflected who we were as a couple in the later stages of our lives, we were beset with health challenges. Wispa, unfortunately, was not exempt from these either. Thankfully, after undergoing extensive treatment she is now cancer-free and making our hearts smile every day with her intelligence, love and affection and believe it or not her sense of humour too!

I will let Wispa introduce herself in her own words on one of two blogs she wrote on my website at www.sandraemanning.com. Where chocolate lovers can also see pictures of our favourite soft centre.

Ooookay puppy lovers...my name is Wispa. I am 12 weeks old and standing in for my mum today here on her blog. As you can see from my pictures, I am pretty flippin' cute and although I say it myself my dribble is much more entertaining than my mum's. Keep that one under your puppy training pads, though, because I am still learning the combination to the snack cupboard.

I was born on April Fool's Day, but I think my mum is a lot more foolish than me because she always falls for my puppy eyes routine every time I do something naughty. All I have to do is flatten my ears, assume the pity position and she is putty in my paws.

Before I came to live in my new house I used to live on a farm in Wales and at first, I was very sad to leave it, but I am getting used to all the new sights and smells in my new home...or I was.

Disaster struck earlier this week and whilst I was enjoying playing with my toys, I suddenly felt a sharp pain in my back leg – boy *did that hurt! My mum whisked me off to the vet and they put me to sleep so that they could take some pictures of the bones in my leg, not my best feature to be honest. As it turns out one of the bones in my leg was broken. The guys at the vets must have been born on the 1st of April too, because they couldn't get enough of my puppy dog eyes and tail wagging routine either. I had to quit that, though, when they kept saying they wanted to keep me, because I wanted to get home. At first, they thought I would need something called an operation? But the orthopaedic vet said my leg would get better with some strict cage rest.*

So now I have to rest my leg and not play with my toys or run around, which is a shame, because I was getting pretty speedy and really enjoyed watching my mum try to catch up with me. She pants more than I do.

I don't know how long I have to stay in prison. No one will tell me, but I can tell you it's getting very boring in here. Still, my mum and dad seem pretty pleased that I have learned that they don't seem to like their carpets wet, and I shout to them now when I want to go to the toilet. You should see how crazy they get when I pooh outside, they sure seem to love their shagpile.

Still, writing this blog is helping me to pass the time in solitary confinement. I don't know what Mum finds so hard about writing hers. It's pretty straightforward once you have learned how to paws for good effect.

Wow! It's nearly labracadabrador time already. I need to start my poorly paw whimper so that Mum will spring me from my crate and put some of that painkiller stuff on my pooched eggs, works like magic every time. Humans are so predictable.

If anyone would like me to take over this blog from my Mum from time to time just leave me a comment and a treat (preferably chicken flavour) and I'll be happy to yap with you again soon. Love from Wispa.

Still Taking The Fight To The Challenge

Life is still a challenge for Craig, in that his health continues to deliver them on a regular basis. Thankfully, up to press, the results of the tests and surgeries he has undergone associated with these challenges have fallen, so far, in his favour. This doesn't mean that the effects of his conditions are not something he battles with every day, but he does so with a smile on his face and a determination to keep all of his well-earned bragging rights that are so important to his claims of invincibility. I have nothing but admiration for a man whose instinct is always to fight back harder and stronger.

Leyla Mae Bell – 02.09.2021 to 14.01.2023

As I already know, and as I suspect those of you drawn to either of my books because of their titles will also know, sometimes it doesn't matter how hard you fight because some battles remain beyond the grasp of victory regardless. Almost two years after Craig and I celebrated our wedding our beautiful granddaughter Leyla Mae made her entrance into the world.

I have witnessed countless acts of bravery during a lifetime of having the unenviable vantage point of many a hospital bedside. Seldom, however, have I seen courage like that shown by my beautiful granddaughter. Thanks to her brief but enduring presence much has been learned to help babies who wait for the gift of a donor heart that for her, unfortunately, never came.

Craig and I visited the Freeman Hospital in Newcastle where Leyla spent much of her short life many times and I hope she knows that I meant everything I said during our last visit, which was also the last time that I saw her.

The following is a blog that I wrote about Leyla on my website at www.sandraemanning.com where anyone who wishes to do so can also view pictures of our beloved granddaughter.

Leyla The Baby With A Broken Heart

I thought I knew and understood heartbreak. After all, you probably can't write a book with a title such as ***The Funny Thing About Being a Widow?*** *unless you possess a hard-earned degree in devastation.*

Although, I truly believed after losing my husband that my heart had broken beyond repair, the resilient, hard-working organ in my chest continued to beat, never losing the capacity to heal by itself, which over time is exactly what it did.

When my beautiful granddaughter Lelya came into our lives almost a year ago, this time my heart melted into a pool of molten love as she immediately took her rightful place inside of it. However, the feelings of elation and joy which come with the birth of a treasured new life, in our case, were not ours for long. After a few blissful weeks during which our little girl showed that she was already a force to be reckoned with, Leyla was diagnosed with serious and life-threatening problems with her heart. With the exception of those first three weeks after she was born, she has never known a life outside of a hospital environment.

Leyla is reliant on a Berlin heart device to keep her alive until she can have a heart transplant that will hopefully give her the chance of life. This beautiful baby girl, who can't even make a sound because of her tracheostomy, still finds ways to let it be known that she wants her shot at a normal life and will fight as hard as she can to be given it. Would you believe that the baby sitting up in the first picture had suffered a stroke? No, neither would I until I felt my heart break again when I learned that she had.

I have left the provision of all the details of Leyla's remarkable fight for life with the inspiration that is her mother Savana Bell. There is no one better placed to communicate their story than her, whose strength borders on the superhuman at times. You can read her posts on the ***Voices from Another Mother*** *by using the following link.*
https://sandraemanning.com/**voices-from-anot...ther-savana-bell/**

Unfortunately, Leyla is in need of a transplant now more than ever after her condition has deteriorated recently. The whole family, are all too well aware of the fact that Leyla's chance of life can only come at the cost of the tragedy that will be the loss of another young life for another family. But for those wonderful families who are able to contemplate the gift of organ donation at the most difficult of times can take comfort from knowing that their bravery might help Leyla and many other children just like her.

As my followers know, I have offered my musings into the ether usually intending to try to put a smile on someone's face, however, briefly. This time the mission could not be more serious or important. I have often heard about the power of social media, but my limited experience of the corner occupied by yours truly is that unless you have pneumatic lips and eyebrows that enter the room before the rest of you, a prosthetic bum like a shelf or some other form of mind-boggling body augmentation, the likes and shares are in short supply.

Well, my granddaughter has a form of bodily augmentation too...it's called a Berlin Heart and it has been a lot more useful than any of the aforementioned enhancements. So, can we please get liking and sharing?

Show me the real meaning of the power of social media...maybe...just maybe... this or Savana's post will reach the person in charge of the department for miracles so that we can get Leyla home to her family where she rightfully belongs.

Goodbye Darling Girl

Leyla Mae Bell died in the arms of her doting parents on the 14th of January 2023. Words will never be enough to express what she meant to all of us who loved her, so I am not even going to try. I will only add that amongst my most abiding memories of our darling Leyla are her wonderful smile, which literally lit up the whole room, and her infectious giggle. They showed just how much she loved life, even one spent for the most part within the confines of a hospital environment. Whenever I close my eyes, I can see her surrounded by the books she loved to read with her mum, her curious nature evident even then and which I am sure would have propelled her to the brightest of futures, had she lived.

Leyla's name will live on in the work done by the #TheLeylaMaeFoundation, which is a charity set up by her mum Savana to help families of children like Leyla, who face long hospital stays, which can be financially devastating for them.

I know, too, that it is Leyla's parent's greatest wish that the conversation concerning organ donation, especially, in babies and young children, is had more openly, despite the obvious difficulties in doing so.

Sleep well, my darling baby girl, our lives are so much richer for having known and loved you.

Chapter 11

In Conclusion

Things As I See Them

As I look back now at the time I spent on dating sites, I can say without fear of contradiction that they are difficult places to negotiate and it requires diligence to do so safely. We have already covered at length the hazards you might encounter on a dating site, such as the *romance fraudsters,* who unfortunately form not only part of this particular landscape but increasingly that of many other social media platforms too. Hopefully, this information will prove useful to help identify the red flags that should alert us to the presence of this particular group. Even when we have navigated ourselves away from the site towards what we hope will be, at the very least, the acquisition of a friend, if not a lifelong partner, the potential to be harmed does not cease to exist.

What I did not appreciate properly when I began my exploration of dating sites was the true extent of my vulnerability as a widow. Now that I am fortunate to be enjoying life again with a kind and loving husband, I hardly recognise the person who wrote about her experiences in the way that I have. I realise now, though, that my behaviour was symptomatic of someone who preferred to live with the pain she could inflict on herself, rather than face the pain caused by losing the husband she adored. This caused me to be vulnerable in ways I hadn't thought possible and this needs to be acknowledged and understood by every widow or widower contemplating the use of a dating site.

Everything I have written in this book is offered from an entirely personal perspective. For me to try and create any kind of balance between the negatives and the positives of internet dating at this juncture, that is not entirely reflective of that experience, would seem to me to be less than authentic.

Down To Business

When we inform ourselves properly about the risks of any activity that we are considering, we can hopefully then use this information to assess any potential risks in light of our individual needs. This will inevitably mean that people engaging with the exact same process can experience a different outcome as a result of these assessments.

Where dating sites were concerned, I came to regard them as little more than places where vendors and buyers meet in the hope of conducting a transaction that will prove to be mutually beneficial to both parties. Essentially, they are an advertising platform where the commodity on offer is the promise of something, rather than an actual tangible product. The problems arise when there is a lack of equity in the transactions that take place on these sites. This could be because, as in the case of a *romance fraudster,* they are seeking to gain a financial advantage or because the expectations concerning the scope of a dating site are set artificially high by those who use one. In this context, I would simply like to remind you of the following: *Caveat Emptor quia ignore non debuit quod jus alienum emit*

The literal translation of this is *let a purchaser beware, for they ought not to be ignorant of the nature of the property which they are buying from another party.*

Beer Goggles

When it comes to considering the many ways that we can protect ourselves from coming to any harm on a dating site, negotiating one whilst wearing a pair of beer goggles is ill-advised. I know this to my cost, having used them on more occasions than I can remember, which in itself rather illustrates my point. Drinking to excess at any time is never a good idea, but especially so, when using an online dating site. Alcohol can make you blind to the significance of the Red Flags that you will inevitably encounter. It will also, make you more susceptible to the tactics of flattery used by *romance fraudsters,* which can then expose you to a greater risk of financial manipulation. Not least of these adverse effects is that they can also cause acute embarrassment. There were many *mornings after the night before,* when I was forced to re-read some of the messages, I had sent out into the ether in such gay abandon, and for which I had to apologise profusely the next day.

Dens Of Iniquity?

I do not subscribe to the view that dating sites are nothing more than convenient places for con artists and scammers to ply their stock in trade. I see them described as such in many of the forums of which I am a member, whenever the subject of dating crops up, which is often. Whilst we already know that this particular group inarguably has a considerable presence on dating sites, their membership does not consist entirely of this type of user. They are also frequented, admittedly in smaller numbers, by people who are genuinely searching for another chance at happiness. To blithely assume that this isn't the case is like believing that Earth is the only planet in the Universe on which life forms exist.

Proof of the existence of genuine people who use dating sites legitimately relates directly back to my own experience, although I am aware of many other introductions that also originated on dating sites and resulted in successful partnerships and marriages. Whatever the vagaries of these platforms, you only have to get lucky once for them to deliver life-changing results. People do not think twice about handing their hard-earned cash over in exchange for a lottery ticket or a scratch card, despite knowing that their chances of winning either are next to non-existent.

The Unexpected Benefits

One of the first things that I gained from my presence on a dating site was something I didn't consider as a benefit until I reached this point in the book. Quite simply, the time I spent on dating sites and researching them gave me something to occupy my mind. This might not seem like much of a plus point and might even be viewed as a sad reflection of how empty a life I was leading at the time. This would not only be true but is also exactly my point. Each hour that passed during the time I spent researching dating sites was one less I had to spend in painful contemplation of the irrevocable and sad changes that had occurred in my life. This, as I look back now, can only be regarded as a good thing.

Whilst you might not immediately consider a dating site to be associated with any kind of learning opportunity, I would respectfully beg to differ. I learned many a valuable lesson about human nature and discovered that the best and worst examples exist on a dating site, just as they do in life. I learned much about myself too, that despite my mistakes, and there were many, I was capable of negotiating new and different things. It also taught me much about the kind of men that I did not want or need to be part of any future relationship plans. This was especially useful in light of the way I had been cocooned in nothing but love and respect in my previous existence and was in some ways quite naive about men as a result.

Gradually, I started to use the different elements from all of my experiences, both the good and the bad, to help guide me towards a new and different purpose. It was also at this time that I finally received the long-awaited confirmation that not only was I ready to live the life that I had all but given up on after losing Kenny, but that now I actually wanted to.

I have no way of knowing what I would be doing with my life right now had I not made the choice to use and research dating sites. It is possible, if unlikely, that I might have met someone in the traditional way and that we would have gone on to live happily ever after. In this unlikely scenario, however, I would have missed out on all the valuable lessons that I learned above, which in many ways changed me as a person. I have spent a large part of my life putting the needs of others ahead of my own, to such an extent that I never properly understood what they were until now. Maybe this is just because, at this stage in my life, I am benefiting from the wisdom that comes with age, which is how nature compensates older people for all the things that we have to surrender in return.

The Future

I am not sure what to include under this particular sub-heading. The future is such a subjective entity that we can plan for and try to imagine, but the reality is that I might not even get to finish typing this sentence if fate decides that it is not in my future to do so. I have decided, therefore, to share the following with you, which is something I wrote in my past concerning the wisdom of waiting for one of life's lightbulb moments.

A Lightbulb Moment

The phrase 'lightbulb moment' is designed to convey the arrival of an inspirational thought in all the time it takes to illuminate well... a light bulb. Given that I am running on empty at the moment, with lockdown having robbed me of huge chunks of my confidence, motivation and 'give a shitness' (yes it has affected my use of language too), I decided to research how I might manipulate the laws of attraction to avail myself of such a moment.

The origins of the lightbulb, now a humble household staple, are more ambiguous than you might expect. Most of us are inclined to credit the US inventor Thomas Edison as the person behind the invention of the lightbulb in 1879. In fact, it was the British chemist Warren de La Rue who solved the scientific challenges relating to this concept some 40 years earlier. However, his efforts were not commercially viable and in 1878 another British scientist, Joseph Swan, was able to rectify this with his version of the lightbulb but, in doing so, his adaptations led to the technical issue of rapid burnout. Enter Thomas Edison, who was the first to solve both the economic and scientific challenges of light bulb production. It is clearly evident, however, that there was a huge body of work involved before he was able to reach this point in a process that is still evolving during present times.

If the humble lightbulb was created by a series of moments rather than just one in particular, then I was to discover that the same might also be said of the Eureka moment. A word first uttered by the ancient Greek Archimedes after he suddenly developed an understanding of a previously incomprehensible problem whilst taking a bath. Eureka has become synonymous with that Aha! moment of sudden clarity. Whilst Archimedes wrote a lot about the laws of buoyancy, he never actually penned one word about his Aha! moment in the bathtub. However, some 200 years after this event was presumed to have taken place, it was a Roman named Vitruvius who included the story in his book on architecture. It is possible that Vitruvius either misinterpreted the origins of the story or, that it was simply one of those tales that improved in the telling over a period of time.

Again, it is likely that Archimedes' sudden understanding of a complex concept owed much more to a series of moments, in the same way as those which led to the production of the light bulb. The consequences of this realisation seemed to be much more far-reaching than I had at first supposed. What if a rogue Granny Smith falling onto the head of Isaac Newton was not the exact moment at which he discovered the laws of gravity? Using the same logic is it likely that it took a bit more than a few cows appearing in a dream to help Einstein come up with the following?

'When a man sits with a pretty girl for an hour, it seems like a minute. But let him sit on a hot stove for a minute it's longer than any hour. That's relativity.'

Am I then to conclude that I have wasted an inordinate amount of time waiting for that lightbulb or Eureka moment to arrive when in reality no such thing exists? As a writer, I scour the internet daily searching for inspiration, only to end up afflicted with unbridled procrastination instead. I have contemplated my naval, breathed more deeply and regularly than a deep-sea diver and have asked the universe to manifest my inner desires to the point of rudeness. The truth is, that even if I did happen to stumble upon a worthy contender that qualifies as a lightbulb or Eureka moment, then it would be only the beginning of the story. In a world that seeks instant gratification and where success is defined by the number of Facebook blue thumbs you can attract, it is easy to forget the efforts that lead up to any sudden onset of clarity. A primary school teacher gave me the following quote many years ago and it is something that has underpinned many of my endeavours ever since.

'success comes not to extraordinary people, but, to ordinary people who achieve extraordinary things'

It also reminds me that I am often guilty of chasing rainbows instead of building the stairways which would allow me to reach them. In a society where we live out our lives in an increasingly virtual sense, we are becoming ever more detached from the core values that seem now, to belong to a much different era. The strong work ethic instilled in me from a very young age competes with a desire to find a route less arduous, even though my heart tells me there is no such path worth travelling.

To conclude, I have discovered two things as I wrote this article. The first is that the lightbulb or Eureka moment is not a singular concept and waiting for the arrival of one is counterproductive to achieving anything worthwhile. The second is that when you combine a flash of inspiration with drive, ambition, tenacity and patience, only then are you likely to arrive at the moment of clarity which we think of as a lightbulb moment. Perhaps this realisation alone is the closest I am ever going to get to a lightbulb moment...for now at least.

When I re-read the above, I am reminded that the life I have now, which took time to emerge from the wreckage of my previous one, is the result of a culmination of many small but meaningful steps. However, misdirected they were at times, each of them helped deliver me to where I am now, rather than any one pivotal moment. One of those steps was the fortuitous decision to persevere with the difficult negotiations of a dating site. Was it worth the effort? I know what my unequivocal answer to this question is. What will yours be?

If you can learn to laugh again, so can you learn to live again

Sandra E Manning

Resources

Please find below a by-no-means-exhaustive list of dating resources. As I have indicated earlier in the book I do not endorse any particular site or app over the other and provide the following for information only.

www.seniorfishdating.co.uk

www.eharmony.co.uk

www.match.co.uk

www.ourtime.co.uk

www.chapter2.app

About the Author

Sandra E Manning is a writer, who inhabits a world that like many of us, she sometimes struggles to make sense of. By re-framing what she see's through the prism of her humour tinted spectacles she is better able to understand, and deal with, both her own environment and that which extends beyond it.

Sandra is currently working on the 3rd book in the **Funny Thing About Being a Widow?** Series about re-marriage and retirement. She is also involved in the development of a new website for widowers/widowers who like her are negotiating life some years after their loss.

You can read Sandra's regular blog on her website:

www.sandraemanning.com

where you will also find links to her Facebook and Goodreads pages.

Gowns-Grieving Overwhelmed Widows Negotiating Stuff can be accessed via a Facebook search for gownsgroup

Printed in Great Britain
by Amazon

46836747R00116